This book belongs to:

_____

# Virgo Daily Horoscope 2025

Author's Note: Time set to Coordinated Universal Time Zone (UT±0)

Mystic Cat
Suite 41906, 3/2237 Gold Coast HWY
Mermaid Beach, Queensland, 4218
Australia
islandauthor@hotmail.com

# Contents

# The 12 Zodiac Star Signs

# 2025

## January

| S | M | T | W | T | F | S |
|---|---|---|---|---|---|---|
|   |   |   | 1 | 2 | 3 | 4 |
| 5 | 6 | 7 | 8 | 9 | 10 | 11 |
| 12 | 13 | 14 | 15 | 16 | 17 | 18 |
| 19 | 20 | 21 | 22 | 23 | 24 | 25 |
| 26 | 27 | 28 | 29 | 30 | 31 |   |

## February

| S | M | T | W | T | F | S |
|---|---|---|---|---|---|---|
|   |   |   |   |   |   | 1 |
| 2 | 3 | 4 | 5 | 6 | 7 | 8 |
| 9 | 10 | 11 | 12 | 13 | 14 | 15 |
| 16 | 17 | 18 | 19 | 20 | 21 | 22 |
| 23 | 24 | 25 | 26 | 27 | 28 |   |

## March

| S | M | T | W | T | F | S |
|---|---|---|---|---|---|---|
|   |   |   |   |   |   | 1 |
| 2 | 3 | 4 | 5 | 6 | 7 | 8 |
| 9 | 10 | 11 | 12 | 13 | 14 | 15 |
| 16 | 17 | 18 | 19 | 20 | 21 | 22 |
| 23 | 24 | 25 | 26 | 27 | 28 | 29 |
| 30 | 31 |   |   |   |   |   |

## April

| S | M | T | W | T | F | S |
|---|---|---|---|---|---|---|
|   |   | 1 | 2 | 3 | 4 | 5 |
| 6 | 7 | 8 | 9 | 10 | 11 | 12 |
| 13 | 14 | 15 | 16 | 17 | 18 | 19 |
| 20 | 21 | 22 | 23 | 24 | 25 | 26 |
| 27 | 28 | 29 | 30 |   |   |   |

## May

| S | M | T | W | T | F | S |
|---|---|---|---|---|---|---|
|   |   |   |   | 1 | 2 | 3 |
| 4 | 5 | 6 | 7 | 8 | 9 | 10 |
| 11 | 12 | 13 | 14 | 15 | 16 | 17 |
| 18 | 19 | 20 | 21 | 22 | 23 | 24 |
| 25 | 26 | 27 | 28 | 29 | 30 | 31 |

## June

| S | M | T | W | T | F | S |
|---|---|---|---|---|---|---|
| 1 | 2 | 3 | 4 | 5 | 6 | 7 |
| 8 | 9 | 10 | 11 | 12 | 13 | 14 |
| 15 | 16 | 17 | 18 | 19 | 20 | 21 |
| 22 | 23 | 24 | 25 | 26 | 27 | 28 |
| 29 | 30 |   |   |   |   |   |

## July

| S | M | T | W | T | F | S |
|---|---|---|---|---|---|---|
|   |   | 1 | 2 | 3 | 4 | 5 |
| 6 | 7 | 8 | 9 | 10 | 11 | 12 |
| 13 | 14 | 15 | 16 | 17 | 18 | 19 |
| 20 | 21 | 22 | 23 | 24 | 25 | 26 |
| 27 | 28 | 29 | 30 | 31 |   |   |

## August

| S | M | T | W | T | F | S |
|---|---|---|---|---|---|---|
|   |   |   |   |   | 1 | 2 |
| 3 | 4 | 5 | 6 | 7 | 8 | 9 |
| 10 | 11 | 12 | 13 | 14 | 15 | 16 |
| 17 | 18 | 19 | 20 | 21 | 22 | 23 |
| 24 | 25 | 26 | 27 | 28 | 29 | 30 |
| 31 |   |   |   |   |   |   |

## September

| S | M | T | W | T | F | S |
|---|---|---|---|---|---|---|
|   | 1 | 2 | 3 | 4 | 5 | 6 |
| 7 | 8 | 9 | 10 | 11 | 12 | 13 |
| 14 | 15 | 16 | 17 | 18 | 19 | 20 |
| 21 | 22 | 23 | 24 | 25 | 26 | 27 |
| 28 | 29 | 30 |   |   |   |   |

## October

| S | M | T | W | T | F | S |
|---|---|---|---|---|---|---|
|   |   |   | 1 | 2 | 3 | 4 |
| 5 | 6 | 7 | 8 | 9 | 10 | 11 |
| 12 | 13 | 14 | 15 | 16 | 17 | 18 |
| 19 | 20 | 21 | 22 | 23 | 24 | 25 |
| 26 | 27 | 28 | 29 | 30 | 31 |   |

## November

| S | M | T | W | T | F | S |
|---|---|---|---|---|---|---|
|   |   |   |   |   |   | 1 |
| 2 | 3 | 4 | 5 | 6 | 7 | 8 |
| 9 | 10 | 11 | 12 | 13 | 14 | 15 |
| 16 | 17 | 18 | 19 | 20 | 21 | 22 |
| 23 | 24 | 25 | 26 | 27 | 28 | 29 |
| 30 |   |   |   |   |   |   |

## December

| S | M | T | W | T | F | S |
|---|---|---|---|---|---|---|
|   | 1 | 2 | 3 | 4 | 5 | 6 |
| 7 | 8 | 9 | 10 | 11 | 12 | 13 |
| 14 | 15 | 16 | 17 | 18 | 19 | 20 |
| 21 | 22 | 23 | 24 | 25 | 26 | 27 |
| 28 | 29 | 30 | 31 |   |   |   |

# 2025

## Daily Horoscope

**VIRGO**

As your astrologer, I wish to explain why one horoscope book may differ from another for each zodiac sign. The vast array of astrological activity constantly occurring in the sky requires me to focus on the essential aspect of the star sign I am writing for on any given day. Each zodiac sign is unique, and the various planetary factors affect them differently.

When crafting horoscopes, I pay special attention to the significant astrological aspects directly impacting a specific sign. By doing so, I can provide the most insightful and relevant guidance to individuals of that zodiac sign. While there might be multiple planetary alignments on a particular day, one aspect may hold more significance for a specific sign than others.

Considering the ruling planets and elements associated with each zodiac sign further refines my interpretations. This attention to detail ensures that the horoscope resonates with the distinct characteristics and tendencies of the star sign in question.

Ultimately, I aim to offer personalized insights and advice based on each zodiac sign's unique cosmic influences. By focusing on each star sign's most relevant astrological aspects, I can help readers better understand themselves and navigate the energies surrounding them. Embracing each zodiac sign's strengths, challenges, and opportunities allows me to create a horoscope book tailored to my readers' needs.

"We are born at a given moment, in a given place, and, like vintage years of wine, we have the qualities of the year and the season of which we are born. Astrology does not lay claim to anything more."

—Carl Jung

# January

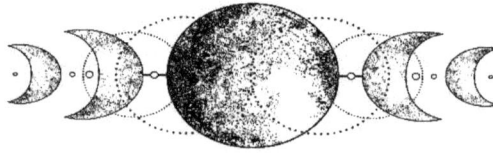

MOON MAGIC

| Sun | Mon | Tue | Wed | Thu | Fri | Sat |
|-----|-----|-----|-----|-----|-----|-----|
|     |     |     | 1   | 2   | 3   | 4   |
| 5   | 6   | 7   | 8   | 9   | 10  | 11  |
| 12  | 13  | 14  | 15  | 16  | 17  | 18  |
| 19  | 20  | 21  | 22  | 23  | 24  | 25  |
| 26  | 27  | 28  | 29  | 30  | 31  |     |

# NEW MOON

---

# WOLF MOON

**30 Monday**

With the Moon ingress Capricorn and the arrival of the New Moon, you may feel a strong sense of determination and ambition. Your focus may shift towards long-term plans and responsibilities as you seek to establish a solid foundation for your future. It's a favorable period to embrace discipline and perseverance as you lay the groundwork for success. This New Moon offers growth and personal development opportunities, and you can enjoy the journey toward your goals.

**31 Tuesday**

You open a journey that takes you to an emotionally abundant chapter. It does rejuvenate your personal life as you deepen a romantic bond that lights up pathways of growth and inspiration. It brings romance and magic into your life. A sense of synchronicity and serendipity tells of blessings and a meaningful journey in your life. It lights the way forward that promotes happiness and harmony.

**1 Wednesday**

On New Year's Day, with the Moon ingress Aquarius, excitement and innovation fill the air. This lunar influence encourages you to break free from old patterns and embrace individuality. It's an excellent time to set intentions for the year ahead and to cultivate a vision of a future filled with progress and positive change. As you enter the new year, allow the energy of Aquarius to inspire you to be true to yourself and contribute to the collective in meaningful and inventive ways.

**2 Thursday**

Life brims with possibility as you chart a course toward development. Negotiating advancement brings a focus on growing life outwardly. It seals the deal to improving your life. Rising motivation attracts inspiration and confidence that helps you gain traction on your goals. You gain access to a prosperous environment that is key to future growth. You touch down on a landscape ripe with opportunity. It triggers a cascade of new options for your life.

### 3 Friday

As the Moon enters Pisces, you may feel an emotional shift, heightening your intuition and imagination. This emotionally charged alignment is a time to trust your instincts and explore your creative pursuits. Allow yourself to dive deep into emotions and seek solace in artistic expressions. Embrace the energy of Venus in Pisces, navigate the intensity of Mars as opposed to Pluto, and let the Moon in Pisces guide you toward a more compassionate and intuitive way of being.

### 4 Saturday

With the Sun forming a sextile with Saturn, you can bring discipline, structure, and focus into your life. This harmonious alignment encourages you to take responsibility for your actions, set realistic goals, and work diligently towards achieving them. You can establish a solid foundation for long-term success and stability. This aspect brings a sense of purpose and determination, allowing you to overcome obstacles and persevere.

### 5 Sunday

With the Moon's ingress into Aries, you feel a surge of energy and a renewed sense of motivation. This fiery and assertive energy inspires you to take a proactive approach. It's a time to trust your instincts, follow your passions, and boldly pursue your goals. You may crave independence and freedom, eager to break from limitations or constraints. This lunar transit encourages you to be courageous, take the initiative, and embrace new beginnings.

### 6 Monday

Mercury square Neptune may bring some confusion and challenges in communication. You might find it difficult to express your thoughts and ideas, leading to misunderstandings. Adopting active listening and taking extra care when making important decisions is helpful. Remain open to alternative perspectives and be mindful of potential deception or illusions. Trust your intuition and verify facts to ensure accuracy and avoid unnecessary complications.

### 7 Tuesday

With the Moon entering Taurus, you may experience a shift towards seeking stability, comfort, and sensual pleasures in your life. Your emotions are grounded, and you draw simple joys of life, such as good food, physical touch, and a cozy atmosphere. You might find solace in connecting with nature, indulging in self-care activities, or spending time with loved ones. Allow yourself to slow down, appreciate the beauty around you, and find peace in the present moment.

### 8 Wednesday

With Mercury entering Capricorn, you may adopt a more practical and disciplined approach and be more inclined to engage in structured conversations and discussions around practical and business-related topics. This transit encourages you to prioritize responsibility, integrity, and practicality in your interactions and mental pursuits. Use this time to develop a solid action plan, set realistic goals, and communicate your ideas clearly and organized.

### 9 Thursday

Transformation on the horizon provides an opportunity to wipe the slate clean. It offers you a real chance to achieve growth and happiness in your life, launching a cycle of increasing possibility that leaves you radiant about future options. Exploring new pathways jumpstart a period of growth and prosperity, enabling you to push back the barriers and head toward uncharted territory, where you'll discover a golden avenue.

**10 Friday**

With the Moon ingress Gemini, you may feel inclined to communicate your feelings and thoughts with others, sharing ideas and seeking social interaction. It is a time of increased mental activity and a heightened need for mental stimulation. You may find yourself drawn to learning, reading, or engaging in conversations that expand your knowledge. It's important to stay open-minded and flexible, as your emotions may change quickly, and your interests may shift.

**11 Saturday**

The shifting scene overhead fills you with excitement, introducing a social aspect replete with opportunities to mingle. Expanding your social circle encourages a more interconnected and supportive milieu. It ushers in a lively and active period of social engagement, resonating as you embark on a chapter filled with vibrant discussions—invitations to circulate foster spirited dialogues and opportunities to forge deeper connections.

**12 Sunday**

The Moon ingress Cancer/Mars trine Neptune combo sees your intuition guide actions, as you have a heightened ability to understand and support others on an emotional level. It encourages you to pursue dreams and passions with gentle determination, allowing your creative and spiritual energies to flow effortlessly. You may find that your actions align with your deepest values, and you can progress significantly in areas that bring you fulfillment and a sense of purpose.

### 13 Monday

The combination of the Sun trine Uranus and the Full Moon invites you to embrace your individuality and trust in the transformative power of letting go. Allow yourself to be guided by your intuition and the electric energy in the air as you step into a new chapter of personal growth and liberation. It is a time of heightened emotions and a culmination of efforts. Reflect on what you need to let go of to move forward and embrace the fullness of your potential.

### 14 Tuesday

With the Moon entering Leo and Venus forming a square with Jupiter, you are entering a vibrant and expressive phase with the potential for joy and excess. The Moon in Leo ignites your inner fire, fueling your creativity, confidence, and desire for self-expression. However, with Venus square Jupiter, it's essential to be mindful of overindulgence and extravagance. There is a tendency to seek pleasure, which can lead to excess and the temptation to overextend yourself.

### 15 Wednesday

A proactive stance reshapes the landscape as you progress through a realm brimming with potential. It affords you an opportunity to refine and elevate your talents. Rising prospects beckon progress, spurring you to continue evolving and enhancing your abilities as novel horizons beckon you forward. You are rediscovering the magic and potential of harnessing your creativity to craft a blueprint for future growth.

### 16 Thursday

As the Sun opposes Mars and the Moon enters Virgo, you may experience increased tension and a need for precision in your actions. The Sun-opposed Mars aspect can bring forth a clash of wills and a strong desire for assertiveness. It is essential to be mindful of impulsive reactions and potential conflicts during this time. The energy of the Moon's ingress into Virgo complements this aspect by fostering a practical and analytical mindset.

### 17 Friday

The Sun sextile Neptune alignment offers gentle and supportive energy, encouraging you to pursue endeavors that align with your higher purpose. It's a time to trust your intuition and allow your imagination to guide you toward greater fulfillment and spiritual growth. By embracing the mystical energy of this aspect, you can tap into your inner wisdom and create a sense of harmony. Remember to stay grounded as you navigate this calming energy.

### 18 Saturday

Networking ushers in pleasing outcomes as you encounter new companions worthy of your time. A more connected environment infuses your life with a touch of magic. The introduction of insightful individuals into your social life triggers opportunities for collaboration and joint ventures—a more active and productive tempo ushers in pivotal growth. Expanding options cast a spotlight on burgeoning prospects that bestow blessings upon your life.

### 19 Sunday

With Venus conjunct Saturn, you may experience a time of practicality and stability in your relationships and values. This aspect brings a sense of commitment and responsibility to your interactions, encouraging you to approach matters of the heart with maturity and long-term vision. The Moon's ingress into Libra further enhances your focus on creating harmony and balance in your emotional life. You may seek peace and fairness in your relationships today.

### 20 Monday

An exhilarating period ahead ushers in a high note for your social life, attracting unique characters into your world. Sunnier skies loom overhead as you expand your life and enhance your world. You soon find yourself in the company of a friend who brings companionship and shares insightful ideas with you. The construction of stable foundations cultivates a peaceful and tranquil environment, fostering an atmosphere teeming with rising potential.

### 21 Tuesday

With the Sun conjunct with Pluto, you may experience intense and transformative energies influencing your power and self-expression. This aspect invites you to delve into the depths of your being, uncovering hidden truths. It is a time of personal growth and regeneration, where you can release old patterns and embrace your inner strength. As the Moon ingresses Scorpio, it amplifies these transformative energies, bringing emotional depth and intensity to the forefront.

### 22 Wednesday

A fresh possibility springs to life, signifying the way forward. This development accelerates the pace and offers a new slate of potential. It paves the way for a more connected environment marked by communication and support. Your willingness to improve your circumstances ushers in a prosperous era characterized by thoughtful discussions. Strengthening a friendship supports a path of expansion in your life. A productive period establishes foundations that foster growth.

### 23 Thursday

With Mercury trine Uranus, you can tap into your intuition and think outside the box. This aspect enhances your ability to grasp new concepts quickly and make insightful connections. It encourages you to express your thoughts and ideas unconventionally, fostering intellectual growth and stimulating innovative thinking. It offers dynamic energy, intellectual stimulation, and the potential for breakthroughs and creative problem-solving.

### 24 Friday

With the Moon ingress Sagittarius, you may feel optimistic and a thirst for adventure. This aspect brings a fiery and expansive energy that encourages you to broaden your horizons and seek new experiences. You may explore different cultures, beliefs, and philosophies, and you may find yourself eager to embark on journeys of both the physical and intellectual kind. Emotions infuse you with freedom, inspiring you to break from limitations and embrace an expansive view.

### 25 Saturday

Your actions are fueled by a strong sense of purpose and enthusiasm, allowing you to pursue your goals with determination and vitality. This alignment of Venus and Mars ignites a spark of inspiration and encourages you to embrace your passions, whether in love, creativity, or personal endeavors. You are in tune with your desires and can express them assertively and confidently, leading to harmonious outcomes and fulfilling experiences.

### 26 Sunday

Venus sextile Uranus brings the midst of a transitional phase. News arrives, inspiring growth and enabling the exchange of thoughts and ideas with like-minded individuals who appreciate your perspective and value your contributions. Rising creativity sparks a wealth of potential that unveils an array of possibilities. It engenders a social environment that nurtures stable foundations. Opportunities to socialize with friends introduce a joyous chapter.

### 27 Monday

A wave of good news is set to illuminate your career path. It unveils an enterprising chapter that swings open the gates to substantial advancements, making the development of this area worth your time. Rising prospects on the job front are poised to yield favorable results. You embark on the construction of stable foundations, which in turn promote security and nurture a cheerful working environment. It opens the door to a promising journey rife with advancement.

### 28 Tuesday

With Mercury ingress Aquarius, your thoughts and communication take on an innovative and forward-thinking tone. Your mind becomes curious and open to unconventional ideas, and you may draw intellectual pursuits and discussions that challenge the status quo. This placement encourages you to think outside the box and embrace your unique perspective. You will likely express yourself detached and objectively, valuing rationality and intellectual freedom.

### 29 Wednesday

The combination of Mercury conjunct Pluto and the New Moon creates a potent blend of mental empowerment and transformative potential. You can dig deep within yourself, confront your fears, and explore the depths of your mind. Set powerful intentions during this New Moon, harnessing the energy of Mercury and Pluto to manifest profound transformations in your thoughts, communication, and overall life journey.

### 30 Thursday

The Sun trine Jupiter adds an expansive and optimistic touch to your experiences. This harmonious aspect brings opportunities for growth, abundance, and broadening your horizons. You may feel a renewed sense of purpose and enthusiasm. It is an excellent time to pursue your goals, take calculated risks, and explore new territories. Allow yourself to embrace the blessings that come your way, and have faith in your abilities to manifest your desires.

# FEBRUARY

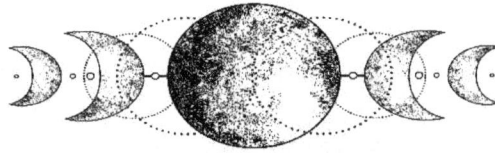

MOON MAGIC

| Sun | Mon | Tue | Wed | Thu | Fri | Sat |
|-----|-----|-----|-----|-----|-----|-----|
|     |     |     |     |     |     | 1   |
| 2   | 3   | 4   | 5   | 6   | 7   | 8   |
| 9   | 10  | 11  | 12  | 13  | 14  | 15  |
| 16  | 17  | 18  | 19  | 20  | 21  | 22  |
| 23  | 24  | 25  | 26  | 27  | 28  |     |

# New Moon

# SNOW MOON

**31 Friday**

A promising chapter emerges as news arrives, casting a bright light on the scope of potential. It opens the door to a journey that steers your life in a fresh direction, ushering in a prosperous period of connecting with your circle of friends. Engaging with your broader community initiates a cascade of options, enabling you to forge ahead in the development of companionship in your life. It dissolves the weight of the past and ushers in lighter, more vibrant energy.

**1 Saturday**

As Venus aligns with Neptune, you are immersed in enchantment and heightened sensitivity. This conjunction invites you to explore love, beauty, and creativity with a touch of dreaminess and imagination. Your heart opens up to deeper connections and spiritual experiences, allowing you to experience love and compassion profoundly. This alignment encourages you to embrace beauty in all life aspects and seek inspiration from art, music, and nature.

**2 Sunday**

With the Moon entering Aries, you feel fiery energy and renewed enthusiasm. This lunar shift ignites your adventurous spirit and fuels your drive to take action. You are ready to tackle challenges head-on and embrace new beginnings with courage and confidence. The Aries Moon empowers you to assert yourself and your needs, pushing you to step out of your comfort zone and embrace your inner warrior.

# FEBRUARY

## 3 Monday

With Mercury forming a harmonious trine aspect to Jupiter, you reveal a brilliant and expansive mind. Your thoughts and ideas flow effortlessly, and you naturally communicate enthusiastically and optimistically. This alignment enhances your intellectual abilities, allowing you to grasp complex concepts and see the bigger picture. Your curiosity and hunger for knowledge heighten, driving you to seek new learning opportunities and expand your horizons.

## 4 Tuesday

As Jupiter shifts direct, its expansive energy encourages growth and forward movement. You may experience renewed optimism, greater purpose, and deepening faith in your abilities. Embrace opportunities, trust your intuition, and take decisive action towards your goals. Embrace the abundant possibilities and allow the harmonious interplay of these cosmic energies to guide you toward success, fulfillment, and joy.

## 5 Wednesday

Rejuvenation prompts reinvention as you explore areas beckoning you to enhance your abilities. It offers you an opportunity to make significant progress in propelling your life forward. By introducing new routines and embarking on visionary projects, you kindle a sense of confidence and excitement. This vibrant start marks a significant turning point, unleashing dormant ideas and allowing them to germinate and flourish.

## 6 Thursday

Embrace the versatility and flexibility that Gemini Moon brings, as it allows you to navigate different situations and adapt to changing circumstances. This lunar transit is a period that encourages you to express your thoughts and ideas, engage in light-hearted communication, and nurture connections with those around you. Let your curiosity guide you as you embark on this dynamic and mentally stimulating phase.

### 7 Friday

With Venus forming a sextile aspect to Pluto, transformative energy infuses your relationships and desires. This alignment deepens your connections on an emotional level, fostering intense intimacy and a profound sense of passion. You may experience a heightened attraction and strong magnetic pull towards a specific situation or experience. This aspect empowers you to delve into the depths of your emotions, allowing you to understand your desires and motivations.

### 8 Saturday

Moon ingress Cancer. Your sensitivity and empathy heighten, allowing you to connect more deeply with others and offer support and understanding. Take time to nurture yourself, create a comforting environment, and surround yourself with people who provide emotional stability. Trust the ebb and flow of your emotions during this lunar transit, knowing they hold valuable insights and guidance for your personal growth.

### 9 Sunday

Mars trine Saturn. You are driven and determined to tackle tasks and pursue your goals with focused effort. This aspect supports structured planning and strategic action, enabling you to make steady progress toward your ambitions. Harness this powerful combination of this celestial influence to assert yourself, communicate effectively, and take purposeful steps toward your objectives. Trust in your abilities and embrace the opportunities for growth and achievement.

**10 Monday**

As the Moon enters Leo, you discover vibrant and confident energy. Your emotions are more expressive and passionate, inspiring you to shine your light and embrace your individuality. This transit is a time to embrace your inner fire and tap into your creativity and leadership abilities. You exude a natural charisma that draws others towards you, and your warm-hearted nature fosters a sense of generosity and kindness in your interactions.

**11 Tuesday**

The Sun square Uranus invites you to embrace your inner rebel and explore new possibilities. However, it's essential to approach this energy with caution, as it can also bring sudden changes and upheavals that require adaptability and resilience. Use this aspect as an opportunity to harness your inner strength and courage and to embrace the excitement and growth that can come from embracing the unexpected.

**12 Wednesday**

Full Moon. This potent lunar phase offers an opportunity for introspection, deep healing, and making necessary adjustments to align with your authentic self. It's a time to honor your emotions, express gratitude, and gain insights into the path ahead. Allow the Full Moon's radiant light to guide you as you embrace transformation and let go of what no longer resonates with your soul's journey. Use this opportunity to express gratitude for your life's blessings and set intentions.

**13 Thursday**

The Moon in Virgo encourages you to organize, be precise, and be attentive to the details of your life. It's an excellent time to analyze situations, solve problems, and improve. Embrace the earthy energy of Virgo to create order and structure in your surroundings and to nurture your overall sense of balance and well-being. Remember to be gentle with yourself and find joy in refining and perfecting your everyday life.

### 14 Friday

Mercury ingress Pisces is a time to embrace the power of words and use them to convey the depth of emotions. Allow your intuition to guide your conversations and interactions as you tap into the subtler nuances of love and connection. This transit encourages you to listen openly and express your feelings with grace and tenderness. It's a beautiful opportunity to strengthen existing relationships, cultivate connections, and create memories filled with love and romance.

### 15 Saturday

Moon ingress Libra. It's a time to foster connections, engage in meaningful conversations, and cultivate peace in your interactions. You may feel a greater desire for beauty and aesthetics, appreciating the finer things in life and seeking out experiences that bring joy and harmony. Embrace the graceful energy of Libra as you navigate your relationships and the world with a sense of grace and diplomacy.

### 16 Sunday

Opportunity arrives unannounced, bearing news that rekindles optimism and happiness. It invites a transition into a social realm that fills you with joy, where engaging conversations with friends keep you in your most pleasing element. Pursuing your goals welcomes a positive influence, brightening your mood as supportive friends contribute insights and camaraderie, paving the way for a bright and breezy period ahead.

### 17 Monday

New potential charts a meaningful course forward in your life. Incoming news promises a significant boost and enhances the potential of your social life. A lively period for sharing with friends unfolds, orienting you toward deepening personal bonds that support your life. This upbeat vibe infuses your closest relationships with renewed energy, driving you to continue bonding and sharing with friends. A gentle shift facilitates concrete progress in achieving growth and happiness.

### 18 Tuesday

With the Sun's ingress into Pisces, gentle and compassionate energy envelops you, encouraging you to tap into your intuitive and empathetic nature. This period highlights the importance of connection, empathy, and unconditional love. You may feel a heightened sense of spiritual connection and a greater sensitivity to the emotions of others. Allow yourself to be guided by your intuition and trust in the flow as you navigate the depths of your feelings and this time's mystical energy.

### 19 Wednesday

Expanding your horizons widens the array of doors for your world to grow. Continually developing new ideas ensures a steady evolution of your talents. Thriving on new challenges elevates your abilities. Collaborating with friends on a group project adds a standout dimension to your growth. A rising aspect unveils success on the horizon, with strategizing and thinking enabling you to transform and learn.

### 20 Thursday

As the Moon enters Sagittarius and Mercury forms a square aspect with Jupiter, you may feel a surge of restless energy and a desire for expansion and exploration. Sagittarius's influence ignites your adventurous spirit, urging you to seek new experiences and broaden your horizons. You can break from limitations and embrace an expansive view. However, with Mercury square Jupiter, there may be a tendency to excessive optimism or overconfidence in your ideas and beliefs.

**21 Friday**

News arrives, casting light on a creative endeavor that opens the door to expanding your skills. Engaging with friends and hatching plans for future growth amplifies your sense of fulfillment and excitement. It affords you a chance to nurture a journey founded on stable foundations, creating a gateway for involvement in a group project and progress in your abilities. Riding a wave of hopeful energy, you embrace lightness and momentum in your social life.

**22 Saturday**

The Capricorn Moon reminds you of the importance of structure and organization in your daily routine. It urges you to assess your priorities and make wise decisions that align with your long-term aspirations. Embrace the diligent and determined spirit of Capricorn as you work towards your goals, knowing that perseverance and a strong work ethic will lead to steady progress and eventual fulfillment. By harnessing the energy of Capricorn, you can make strides toward your goals.

**23 Sunday**

Life heats up with potential, setting the stage for you to thrive in a social environment teeming with opportunities to interact with friends. A glimpse of a path that supports your dreams emerges, ushering in people who play a meaningful role and offer supportive energy to foster new friendships and collaboration. The result is an energetic, joy-filled journey with a fresh outlook. A bustling period awaits you, with your schedule filling up.

**24 Monday**

Mars turns direct is an opportune time to direct your energy towards projects, tasks, and pursuits that may have felt stagnant or on hold. Harness the fiery power of Mars to assert yourself, pursue your passions, and make significant progress in areas that matter to you. With Mars in direct motion, you can make considerable progress. Trust in your inner drive and use this forward motion of Mars to propel yourself toward success and achievement.

**25 Tuesday**

Moon ingress Aquarius. Mercury conjunct Saturn. Your communication style may take on a more serious and structured tone, allowing you to express yourself with clarity and authority. It's a time to tap into your intellectual prowess and engage in academic pursuits or problem-solving activities. Embrace the innovative energy of Aquarius and the meticulous nature of Mercury conjunct Saturn to bring about productive and insightful outcomes in your endeavors.

**26 Wednesday**

Your perseverance and dedication propel you toward progress in your career path. It facilitates pushing past the barriers, advancing your life further by venturing into a new realm. Developing your skills initiates a busy period of learning and growth, enabling you to explore uncharted territories and emerge victorious. Enhanced stability empowers you to plan your path forward, lighting the way for advancement as your skills shine brightly.

**27 Thursday**

Mercury sextile Uranus. This aspect supports unique and out-of-the-box thinking, allowing you to express yourself in unconventional ways. It's an excellent time to engage in intellectual pursuits, explore new concepts, and enthusiastically communicate your ideas. Embrace the harmonious blend of intuitive and intelligent energies during this phase, as it empowers you to navigate the world with a fresh perspective and uncover hidden possibilities.

# MARCH

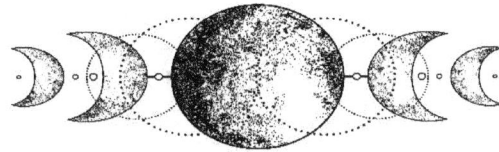

MOON MAGIC

| Sun | Mon | Tue | Wed | Thu | Fri | Sat |
|-----|-----|-----|-----|-----|-----|-----|
|     |     |     |     |     |     | 1   |
| 2   | 3   | 4   | 5   | 6   | 7   | 8   |
| 9   | 10  | 11  | 12  | 13  | 14  | 15  |
| 16  | 17  | 18  | 19  | 20  | 21  | 22  |
| 23  | 24  | 25  | 26  | 27  | 28  | 29  |
| 30  | 31  |     |     |     |     |     |

# NEW MOON

# WORM MOON

**28 Friday**

Take time to clarify intentions, visualize dreams, and take proactive steps toward their manifestation. Embrace the energy of new beginnings and allow yourself to be guided by intuition as you embark on this transformative journey. Trust in the infinite possibilities and believe in your ability to create the life you envision. The New Moon is a powerful time for intention setting and self-renewal, providing the perfect opportunity to start afresh and align with the cosmic rhythms of creation.

**1 Saturday**

You may find yourself drawn to new adventures, challenges, and opportunities that test your courage and push you out of your comfort zone. Allow the energy of Aries to inspire you to be bold, proactive, and unafraid to carve your path. With the Moon in Aries, you can initiate change and make things happen. Embrace this fiery energy and let it propel you toward your dreams and aspirations. It's a time to trust your instincts and boldly move forward confidently.

**2 Sunday**

The Sun square Jupiter brings a sense of tension between expansion and practicality. It would be best to balance pursuing your goals and maintaining a grounded perspective. Take this opportunity to reassess your beliefs, adjust your plans, and make conscious choices that align with your true purpose. Use this introspective period to gain clarity, deepen your self-understanding, and make necessary adjustments in your relationships and life path.

# MARCH

**3 Monday**

With Mercury's ingress into Aries, your thoughts and communication take on a more direct and assertive tone. You may feel more decisive and ready to take action on your ideas and plans. This energy encourages you to speak and express yourself confidently and enthusiastically. Meanwhile, the Moon's ingress into Taurus brings a grounding influence, allowing you to find comfort and stability in the practical aspects of life.

**4 Tuesday**

Being open to expanding your life's horizons signals the green light to chase your dreams. Prioritizing yourself works like magic for your circumstances, enabling you to tap into manifestation pathways that attract rising prospects. This period bestows gifts and good luck on your life, heralding a time of working with your creativity, where energy flows effortlessly and abundantly, bringing forth a wellspring of blessings.

**5 Wednesday**

You may find yourself drawn to deep conversations and uncovering the underlying motivations behind people's words and actions. It's an excellent time to engage in research, delve into self-reflection, and explore the depths of your mind. Combining the Moon in Gemini and the Mercury sextile Pluto brings a blend of intellectual curiosity and emotional depth, allowing you to navigate conversations and connections with a greater understanding and authenticity.

**6 Thursday**

A welcomed bonus sets the stage for excitement, helping you establish your talents in a new realm that marks a significant ascent on the ladder of success. Professional achievements and tangible feedback follow suit, allowing you to reap the rewards of your year-long efforts. This dynamic environment continues to draw new possibilities into your life, progressively evolving your skills and talents. You explore unique pathways that promote a richer experience.

**7 Friday**

With the Moon transitioning into Cancer, you may experience heightened emotions and a deepened sense of sensitivity. Your focus turns toward creating a nurturing and comforting environment for yourself and those around you. You may find yourself seeking solace in familiar settings and engaging in activities that evoke a sense of emotional security. This lunar phase encourages you to connect with your intuition and consider your needs.

**8 Saturday**

Sun trine Mars is an excellent time to assert yourself and progress towards your aspirations. Trust in your abilities and embrace the dynamic energy flowing through you. Use this harmonious alignment between the Sun and Mars to propel yourself forward, tackling obstacles with resilience and embracing opportunities for growth and achievement. Embrace this powerful synergy between your willpower and vitality, and let it fuel your ambitions and propel you to success.

**9 Sunday**

When the Moon enters Leo, you reveal radiant and charismatic energy. Your emotions become vibrant and expressive, and you seek attention and recognition. You are naturally inclined to shine and be the center of attention, and this lunar transit amplifies that desire. You may feel a surge of confidence and self-assuredness, ready to showcase your unique talents. Your creative expression flourishes, and you have a heightened appreciation for beauty and aesthetics.

### 10 Monday

A surge of novel choices infuses an optimistic vibe into your world. You strike gold as you propel forward and hone your talents. Evolution and growth on this path help you navigate the storms and head toward brighter skies. Nurturing your aspirations yields valuable outcomes that inspire you to enrich your life. Fresh objectives and an inspiring vision enable you to implement practical adjustments that offer burgeoning prospects.

### 11 Tuesday

Your words carry a touch of sweetness and diplomacy, making them more appealing and persuasive. Your mind craves artistic inspiration and an appreciation for beauty. Use this alignment to engage in heartfelt conversations, express your affection for others, and cultivate greater harmony in your relationships. Allow Mercury and Venus's gentle fusion to bring enchantment and elegance to your interactions, creating a space for understanding and connection.

### 12 Wednesday

Moon ingress Virgo and Sun conjunct Saturn alignment encourage you to take a serious approach to your goals and commitments as you recognize the need for stability and perseverance in achieving them. You may feel a stronger sense of duty and a willingness to make the necessary effort to fulfill your ambitions. It is a time for taking stock of your resources, setting realistic goals, and making practical choices that support your long-term success.

### 13 Thursday

A new life phase takes center stage, with progression as the primary theme. It pairs you with opportunities that propel you toward growth and afford room to unleash your creative prowess. This period of learning and adaptation stimulates expansion, compelling you to break new ground and unlock fresh possibilities. An overarching sense of optimism and inspiration guides your path, empowering the surge of potential in your world.

**14 Friday**

The Full Moon illuminates areas of your life that require attention and resolution, offering valuable insights and heightened emotions. It is a time to assess your personal needs and desires while also considering the needs and perspectives of those around you. The Sun's sextile to Uranus adds a touch of excitement and unpredictability to the mix, opening doors to innovative ideas, unique opportunities, and the potential for personal growth.

**15 Saturday**

Mercury turns retrograde. Embrace the opportunity to delve into deeper levels of understanding and gain valuable insights. Take advantage of this retrograde period with self-reflection, revisiting past experiences, and allowing space for personal growth and transformation. By embracing Mercury retrograde's lessons and challenges, you can emerge with a clearer perspective and a renewed sense of direction.

**16 Sunday**

This enriching period ushers in a fresh start as you find yourself immersed in a social environment filled with lively conversations and shared companionship. Limiting beliefs may have hindered your progress, but as you push past these barriers, you unlock a sense of liberation, which opens the gateway to a more abundant landscape in your life. Developments that nurture well-being and happiness take center stage, swiftly moving you into a vibrant phase.

### 17 Monday

Moon ingress Scorpio is an opportunity to transform and release any emotional baggage or attachments that no longer serve you. Allow yourself to embrace the intensity of this lunar phase and explore the depths of your emotions. Trust your instincts and intuition as you navigate the complex terrain of your inner world. This period offers a powerful invitation to dive into the mysteries of your psyche and emerge with a renewed sense of self-awareness and empowerment.

### 18 Tuesday

This bustling period centers around erecting stable foundations and nurturing a progressive growth phase. Unexpected developments bolster the security in your life, illuminating avenues of success and prosperity as you pivot and proceed toward lucrative opportunities worthy of your time. A rejuvenated sense of purpose propels your vision forward with vigor and clarity. The pursuit of your dreams sparks progress as you extend your reach into uncharted areas.

### 19 Wednesday

Moon ingress Sagittarius. Sun conjunct Neptune. During this time, you are encouraged to follow your dreams and pursue your passions with faith and optimism. It expands your emotional horizons and invites you to embrace adventure and optimism. Embrace the unknown and trust in the guidance of your inner compass. Allow yourself to enjoy the world around you, and let your spirit soar as you embark on a journey of discovery and self-transcendence.

### 20 Thursday

A new astrological year begins as the Sun enters Aries and marks the Vernal Equinox. It is a powerful time of renewal and fresh beginnings. You may feel motivated as Aries ignites your spirit and sparks initiative. It's a time to take action, set goals, and confidently assert yourself. The Vernal Equinox brings balance and harmony, as day and night are equal. It's a reminder to find equilibrium in your life and embrace the opportunities for transformation.

### 21 Friday

When Venus forms a sextile aspect with Pluto, it has a powerful and transformative influence on your relationships and personal values. You can delve deep into your emotions and explore the hidden elements of love, intimacy, and desire. This aspect invites you to embrace your inner strength and tap into your magnetism, drawing people and experiences that resonate with your authentic self. Embrace the opportunity to create meaningful and profound connections.

### 22 Saturday

When the Moon ingresses into Capricorn, you may experience a shift towards a more practical and disciplined approach to your emotions and inner world. Capricorn is an earth sign associated with stability, responsibility, and ambition. During this time, you might focus on long-term goals, career aspirations, and the need for structure and organization. You may feel a heightened sense of determination and a desire to achieve tangible results.

### 23 Sunday

When the Sun is conjunct with Venus, you experience a harmonious blend of love, creativity, and self-expression. This alignment brings warm and magnetic energy to your interactions, allowing you to effortlessly connect with others and radiate a sense of charm and attractiveness. You may feel a heightened appreciation for beauty and a desire to indulge in pleasurable experiences. It is a time to celebrate love, passion, and the joy of being alive.

**24 Monday**

Moon ingress Aquarius and Sun conjunct Mercury is a time for intellectual pursuits, brainstorming, and stimulating conversations with others. You may feel a sense of curiosity and openness to new concepts, making it a good time for learning, sharing ideas, and expanding your mental horizons. Embrace the unique qualities of Aquarius and let your mind soar as you connect with others and explore the realms of knowledge and self-expression.

**25 Tuesday**

Mercury sextile Pluto empowers you to captivate others with your words and ideas. You may find yourself drawn to profound and thought-provoking conversations, seeking to uncover the deeper meaning behind various subjects. It is a time for mental transformation as you tap into the power of your intellect and engage in deep, transformative thinking. Embrace this harmonious aspect and allow it to guide you on a profound understanding and growth journey.

**26 Wednesday**

Moon ingress Pisces is a period for exploring your inner world and tapping into your creative and imaginative side. You may feel drawn to artistic pursuits, spiritual practices, or simply seeking solace in quiet reflection. Allow yourself to embrace the fluidity and mystery of Pisces energy, diving into the depths of your emotions and exploring the realm of dreams. Trust your instincts and listen to the whispers of your soul as you navigate this ethereal and introspective phase.

**27 Thursday**

As the Black Moon enters Scorpio and Venus moves into Pisces, a mystical and intense energy permeates your being. You can explore the depths of your emotions and embrace the enigmatic aspects of your existence. With Venus aligning with Neptune, the planet of dreams and illusions, your heart opens to the vast ocean of love and compassion. You may feel a deep yearning for connection and seek to dissolve the boundaries that separate you from others.

**28 Friday**

As the Moon moves into Aries, you may feel a surge of energy and a renewed sense of purpose. Aries is a fiery and assertive sign, igniting your passion and motivating you to take action. This aspect is a time to embrace your inner warrior as you boldly step forward and assert your needs and desires. The Aries Moon inspires you to be courageous and adventurous, encouraging you to pursue new opportunities and embrace challenges confidently.

**29 Saturday**

The New Moon is a moment to tune in to your inner voice and connect with your intuition, which holds the keys to your personal growth and transformation. Embrace the energy of the New Moon as a blank canvas, ready for you to paint your intentions and manifest your heart's desires. Take this opportunity to align your thoughts, emotions, and actions with the vision you hold for yourself. With each New Moon, you can reinvent and create a life that reflects your aspirations.

**30 Sunday**

As the Moon enters Taurus, grounding and stability come into focus, providing a solid foundation for your emotional well-being. You are encouraged to nurture yourself and find comfort in simple pleasures. Trust in the cosmic energies at play, allowing them to guide you toward a deeper understanding of yourself and the world around you. Embrace the intuitive wisdom within and embrace the journey of self-discovery with an open heart and mind.

# APRIL

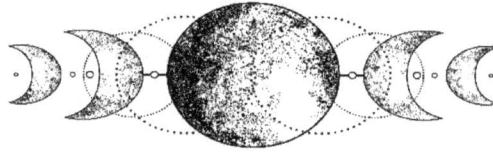

MOON MAGIC

| Sun | Mon | Tue | Wed | Thu | Fri | Sat |
|-----|-----|-----|-----|-----|-----|-----|
|     |     | 1 | 2 | 3 | 4 | 5 |
| 6 | 7 | 8 | 9 | 10 | 11 | 12 |
| 13 | 14 | 15 | 16 | 17 | 18 | 19 |
| 20 | 21 | 22 | 23 | 24 | 25 | 26 |
| 27 | 28 | 29 | 30 |   |   |   |

## NEW MOON

# PINK MOON

### 31 Monday

Change envelops your life, aligning you with new options in both your career and social circles. New possibilities propel you forward, with positive news shedding light on the scope of expansion. It aids in building a stable foundation in your life, a solid base from which to launch new endeavors. It cultivates an environment rich in creativity, ushering in a flourishing chapter. It advances your life by eliminating the barriers that have held you back.

### 1 Tuesday

Moon ingress Gemini. Embrace Gemini energy's versatility and flexibility as you navigate different perspectives and engage in stimulating mental activities. Use this lunar influence to expand your knowledge, clearly express yourself, and connect with others intellectually. Enjoy the playful and curious energy of the Moon in Gemini, and let it inspire you to embrace the joy of learning, connecting, and engaging with the world around you.

### 2 Wednesday

As creativity surges, you gain the opportunity to direct your talents, building prosperity around your life. It permits you to flex your gifts and advance your abilities to the next level. You are prepared to embrace a lighter influence, embarking on a new chapter teeming with hopes and dreams, nurturing fulfillment and happiness. This journey carries you toward joy and harmony. A group project emerges as a fitting addition to your life.

### 3 Thursday

Moon ingress Cancer. You may feel more attuned to the needs and feelings of others, offering a compassionate ear and a supportive presence. It's a time to prioritize self-care, indulge in relaxing activities, and create a safe space to retreat and recharge. Allow the nurturing energy of Cancer to envelop you, reminding you to listen to your intuition and tend to your emotional needs with kindness and compassion.

**4 Friday**

As Saturn sextiles Uranus and Mars sextiles Uranus, you may experience a dynamic interplay between structure and innovation. This cosmic alignment invites you to balance tradition, progress, stability, and change. You can embrace the energy of both planets and harness their unique qualities to your advantage. Saturn's influence brings discipline, structure, and a desire for stability, while Uranus injects a dose of liberation and a willingness to break from conventions.

**5 Saturday**

With Mars forming a trine aspect to Saturn, you may feel a powerful alignment between your drive and ambition and your ability to work methodically. This harmonious connection between these two planets empowers you with discipline, focus, and perseverance to overcome challenges and succeed. You can harness your energy and direct it towards productive endeavors, utilizing your strategic thinking and careful planning to make steady progress.

**6 Sunday**

With the Moon entering Leo, you reveal a vibrant and expressive energy. This celestial shift brings a sense of confidence and enthusiasm to your emotions, allowing you to radiate warmth and charisma in your interactions with others. Coupled with the Sun forming a harmonious sextile with Jupiter, you get a positive and expansive outlook on life. This alignment enhances your optimism, encourages growth, and opens doors to exciting opportunities.

## 7 Monday

When Venus aligns with Saturn in conjunction, you may experience a blending of love, beauty, and discipline in your life. This aspect invites you to bring responsibility and structure to your relationships, artistic pursuits, and financial matters. You may prioritize long-term commitments, seek stability, and make practical choices in heart matters. Venus represents love, harmony, and aesthetics, while Saturn brings a sense of boundaries, commitment, and maturity.

## 8 Tuesday

Venus sextile Uranus. Moon ingress Virgo. You may feel a greater need for order and structure, and this can be a productive time for tackling tasks and responsibilities. Harness the harmonious energy of Venus and Uranus to infuse your relationships and personal values with a sense of adventure and spontaneity. At the same time, let the grounding influence of the Moon in Virgo help you bring clarity and practicality to your emotions and everyday life.

## 9 Wednesday

You are on the cusp of a busy period, where efficiency takes precedence in improving your circumstances. Step by step, you lay the foundations of your life, ensuring they are stable and balanced. The energy of manifestation swirls around your environment, aiding you in turning the corner and taking your life in a new direction. By harnessing your creative abilities, you nurture well-being, significantly enhancing your life.

## 10 Thursday

A river of unique possibilities emerges in your broader social network, serving as a gateway for your life's evolution. A positive influence resonates in your life, ushering new options to your door. Your social schedule fills up with opportunities to mingle, paving the way for progress and possibility. This dynamic period gives rise to lively discussions and opportunities for entertaining with friends.

### 11 Friday

With the Moon's ingress into Libra, you may find yourself drawn towards harmonious interactions, seeking balance, and cultivating a sense of fairness in your relationships and surroundings. This lunar influence encourages you to consider different perspectives, prioritize diplomacy, and find common ground with others. You may have an increased desire for peace and cooperation, valuing compromise and seeking to create a harmonious atmosphere in your interactions.

### 12 Saturday

Your social circle ignites new possibilities, fueling your vibrant and energetic path. New opportunities unfold in a flourish, accelerating your journey toward a fascinating, lively period. Embracing openness to meeting new people widens the realm of possibilities for growth and companionship in your life. As you push back the barriers and focus on nurturing friendships, you dive into a lively and dynamic environment, cultivating a sunny aspect of your life.

### 13 Sunday

With the arrival of the Full Moon, you may experience a culmination of emotions and a heightened sense of awareness. This lunar phase encourages you to reflect on the progress you've made and the intentions you've set in recent weeks. As Venus turns direct, you may feel a shift in matters of the heart and a sense of clarity in your relationships. The Moon's ingress into Scorpio intensifies your emotions, inviting you to delve into your inner world and explore the depths of your desires.

# APRIL

### 14 Monday

A gateway to new opportunities stands wide open, infusing your surroundings with fresh energy and inspiration. As you embark on exciting projects, you'll establish a stable foundation and fuel your creativity. Significant influences guide your path, encouraging growth and a deeper understanding of the world around you. This dynamic period offers an outpouring of ideas and inspiration, drawing you into an active and vibrant phase of life.

### 15 Tuesday

The winds of change are blowing, offering you exciting opportunities to broaden your horizons. A fresh chapter unfolds within your social life, where you'll find happiness and confidence through meaningful connections with friends. An invitation arrives, inviting you to share your thoughts and ideas with kindred spirits, reigniting your social engagement and companionship—the lightness and momentum of positive change return, revitalizing your life's journey.

### 16 Wednesday

As the Moon enters Sagittarius, you may feel a sense of expansion and adventure sweeping through your being. This lunar energy encourages you to embrace new horizons, seek wisdom, and broaden your perspectives. Simultaneously, Mercury's ingress into Aries makes your thoughts and communication style bold, direct, and action-oriented. You may feel a surge of enthusiasm and a desire to assert your ideas confidently.

### 17 Thursday

Mercury conjunct Neptune is a time to trust your inner voice and pay attention to symbolic signs. Your words are poetic and compassionate, and you can convey complex ideas with a touch of mysticism. It's a time to embrace the power of your imagination, listen to the whispers of your soul, and express yourself with depth and sensitivity. Allow the Mercury-Neptune conjunction to guide you on a journey of inspiration and spiritual exploration.

## 18 Friday

You become focused on practical matters, setting clear goals and working diligently towards their achievement. The combination of Mars in Leo and the Moon in Capricorn encourages you to channel your passion into tangible actions and make steady progress toward your aspirations. It's a time for assertiveness, perseverance, and taking charge of your destiny. Trust your abilities, harness your inner strength, and let your ambition propel you toward success.

## 19 Saturday

Sun ingress Taurus. Mars trine Neptune alignment empowers you to pursue your goals with a balanced blend of ambition and inspiration. You can follow your passions, guided by your inner wisdom and a deep sense of purpose. Trust in the power of your imagination and allow it to guide you toward meaningful and fulfilling endeavors. Embrace the gentle energy of Taurus and the transformative influence of Mars trine Neptune as you align with your deepest desires.

## 20 Sunday

This Easter Sunday, a day symbolizing renewal, brings excitement and liberation as Venus forms a harmonious sextile with Uranus. This cosmic alignment encourages you to embrace the unexpected and seek unique experiences that expand your horizons. Your relationships may take on a more adventurous and spontaneous tone, fostering a sense of freedom and individuality. Simultaneously, Mercury forms a sextile with Pluto, empowering you with profound insights.

### 21 Monday

During the challenging alignment of the Sun square Mars, you may experience heightened energy and a strong desire to assert yourself. It is essential to be mindful of potential conflicts or impulsive actions arising from this aspect. There might be a sense of tension or frustration as you navigate through obstacles or clashes of will. Finding constructive outlets for this energy is essential, such as physical exercise or engaging in activities that channel your drive and passion.

### 22 Tuesday

Over the coming cosmic phase, a profound transformation takes shape, setting the stage for future growth in your creative pursuits. This transition marks a significant turning point, igniting your dreams and raising your vision to new heights. Hard work and dedication drive your creative projects to new levels, enabling you to gain traction and achieve your goals. A groundbreaking chapter unfolds, bringing you closer to your creative aspirations.

### 23 Wednesday

As the Moon moves into dreamy Pisces, you may enter a realm of heightened emotions and introspection. This lunar ingress invites you to explore the depths of your subconscious, seeking spiritual and emotional insights. However, the Sun square Pluto aspect adds a touch of intensity to the mix. It signifies a period of potential power struggles, where you may encounter challenges that push you to confront deep-seated fears or hidden aspects of yourself.

### 24 Thursday

As you delve deeper into your future goals, your creativity becomes a wellspring of inspiration, keeping your potential alive. News arrives, casting light on new potential in your social life, further enhancing your happiness and well-being. Contemplating your life's choices helps you gain clarity, paving the way for a breakthrough and opening a gateway to excitement and adventure. You land in an enriching environment that enables you to develop your vision.

### 25 Friday

As Venus aligns with Saturn in conjunction, you may feel a sense of responsibility and seriousness permeating your relationships and aesthetic values. This alignment encourages you to take a more structured and disciplined approach to matters of the heart and your values. It's a time when you may prioritize stability, commitment, and long-term planning in your relationships. The Moon's ingress into Aries adds fiery energy and assertiveness, pushing you to take bold action.

### 26 Saturday

Emphasis on building stability in your home life promises a period of expansion and adds promise to your life. Your social life heats up, offering opportunities for networking and new friendships that can enrich your life in many ways. You discover something special that grants you the time to nurture creative projects that pique your interest. An energizing influence encourages you to break through boundaries and seize every opportunity.

### 27 Sunday

With Mars opposing Pluto, you may feel a heightened intensity and power dynamics. This aspect can bring forth deep-seated emotions, desires, and conflicts that require your attention and resolution. Awareness of power struggles or control issues within yourself and your interactions with others is essential. Simultaneously, as the Moon moves into Taurus and a New Moon occurs, you hold an opportunity for fresh beginnings and grounding energy.

# MAY

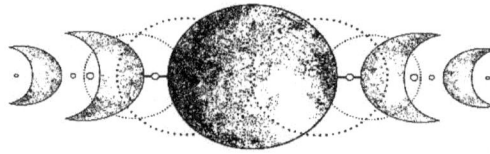

MOON MAGIC

| Sun | Mon | Tue | Wed | Thu | Fri | Sat |
|-----|-----|-----|-----|-----|-----|-----|
|     |     |     |     | 1   | 2   | 3   |
| 4   | 5   | 6   | 7   | 8   | 9   | 10  |
| 11  | 12  | 13  | 14  | 15  | 16  | 17  |
| 18  | 19  | 20  | 21  | 22  | 23  | 24  |
| 25  | 26  | 27  | 28  | 29  | 30  | 31  |

# New Moon

# FLOWER MOON

**28 Monday**

You are on the right track to improve your life. By nurturing your social connections, you'll establish stable foundations to grow your vision. The emphasis on improving your life yields fruitful results. A fantastic journey awaits, one that rewards your planning and willingness to connect with others who support your life—opportunities to mingle open doors to expanding your horizons and building a brighter future.

**29 Tuesday**

Moon ingress Gemini is a time to embrace flexibility and the joy of learning. Use this energy to expand your knowledge, engage in social interactions, and express your thoughts and ideas with clarity and enthusiasm. Your mental faculties are sharp, and you can absorb information swiftly. Allow yourself to embrace Gemini's versatility and open-mindedness, and let your curiosity guide you toward new experiences and connections.

**30 Wednesday**

As Venus enters Aries, you may feel a surge of passion and assertiveness in your relationships and personal desires. Your romantic and social energy becomes more spontaneous and independent, urging you to take the lead and pursue what you truly want. This transit encourages you to be bold and courageous in matters of the heart, expressing your desires and going after what ignites your passion. Embrace the fiery energy of Aries as you confidently pursue your heart's desires.

**1 Thursday**

As the Moon ingresses into Cancer, you may notice a shift in your emotional landscape. Cancer is a nurturing and sensitive sign, and during this time, you may find yourself drawn to activities that bring you comfort and security. Your emotions may become more prominent, and you might feel a greater need for emotional connection and belonging. It's a time to prioritize self-care and tend to your emotional well-being.

# MAY

### 2 Friday

Venus's conjunct Neptune alignment encourages you to tap into your creative expression and engage in activities that allow you to connect with your innermost desires and dreams. It's a time to indulge in the senses' pleasures and let your imagination run wild. Be aware, however, of the need to maintain a grounded perspective. By embracing the magic of Venus conjunct Neptune, you infuse life with wonder and compassion, fostering a deeper connection to beauty and love.

### 3 Saturday

When the Moon enters Leo, you may feel a surge of confidence and self-expression within you. Your inner light shines brightly, and you are ready to take center stage. This transit is a time to embrace individuality, creativity, and passion. You may find yourself craving attention and recognition, seeking opportunities to showcase your unique talents. Your emotions are fiery and enthusiastic, fueling your desire for joy, playfulness, and a sense of adventure.

### 4 Sunday

Pluto's retrograde period encourages you to reflect on your evolution and examine the areas of your life that require healing and regeneration. Embrace the energy of Pluto's retrograde as a catalyst for self-discovery and inner growth, allowing yourself to undergo a powerful metamorphosis that will ultimately lead to greater empowerment and authenticity. Embrace this transformative energy and trust in the growth and evolution process that Pluto retrograde brings forth.

# MAY

**5 Monday**

When Mercury forms a sextile with Jupiter, it brings a harmonious blend of expansive thinking and effective communication. This aspect encourages you to embrace an optimistic mindset, allowing you to see opportunities and possibilities in various parts of your life. You can naturally convey your ideas with confidence and enthusiasm. With the Moon's ingress into Virgo, you may find yourself drawn to practicality and attention to detail.

**6 Tuesday**

Venus's sextile Pluto aspect can bring about a sense of empowerment and personal growth as you navigate the complexities of your connections with others. It's a time for delving into your desires, embracing vulnerability, and fostering emotional intimacy. You may find yourself drawn to intense and passionate experiences, and this aspect can support the transformation and healing of any relationship dynamics.

**7 Wednesday**

Engaging discussions and an expansive chapter emerge, feeling right for your world as you channel your energy into a meaningful area of development. Contemplating your life's choices helps you achieve greater clarity and a breakthrough that leads you toward change. The essence of manifestation fuels your progression toward your goals, creating a brighter chapter as you embark on a cycle of change and evolution, with life supporting your vision for growth.

**8 Thursday**

As the Moon moves into Libra, you may find yourself attuned to this sign's harmonious and diplomatic energies. This transit is when you may naturally seek balance, peace, and cooperation in your interactions with others. You may desire fairness and justice and find yourself mediating conflicts or seeking compromises. Your focus may be on creating harmonious relationships and fostering a sense of unity and understanding.

### 9 Friday

Your finest qualities take the spotlight as a social aspect animates your life. Sharing moments with friends provides essential support, and amidst the shifting sands of life, you find stability within a unique landscape of opportunity. A marvelous trend brings good fortune, introducing you to a new friendship that enhances your expanding circle of exciting options. Engaging conversations and enjoyable outings fill your schedule, making your life lively and social.

### 10 Saturday

As the planet Mercury moves into Taurus, your communication style may take on a more deliberate and grounded tone. You speak with excellent stability and practicality, focusing on fundamental matters and expressing your thoughts steadily and deliberately. This transit encourages you to pay attention to the details and take a measured approach to your words. Meanwhile, with the Moon entering Scorpio, your emotions deepen and intensify.

### 11 Sunday

Improvement around your home and family life brings forth a productive period, nurturing balanced foundations. As you find your groove in a more social environment, your life thrives as a busy time unfolds with a sense of progression and growth. Rising prospects shine a light on new areas worthy of your time, while a golden aspect weaves around your creativity, charting a course for the development of your vision for future growth.

### 12 Monday

Mercury square Pluto aspect invites you to reclaim your power and engage in transformative communication. It is a time to be mindful of power struggles and to approach conversations with sensitivity and authenticity. The Full Moon and Mercury square Pluto combination invites you to embrace the potential for profound change and growth, allowing you to emerge from this transformative period with a deeper understanding of yourself and your relationships.

### 13 Tuesday

When the Moon enters Sagittarius, you may feel a sense of adventure and a desire to explore new horizons. This transit brings renewed optimism and enthusiasm to your emotional landscape. You may find yourself craving freedom and seeking experiences that expand your knowledge and worldview. Your emotions are infused with a spirit of wanderlust, pushing you to venture beyond your comfort zone and embrace new perspectives.

### 14 Wednesday

Your journey includes many valuable gifts to share with the world, particularly when it comes to developing your talents. As you get more involved in honing your skills, unique abilities emerge, offering you ample room for expansion. Your willingness to invest in your abilities sets you on a trajectory of success, elevating various aspects of your life and instilling you with a deep sense of optimism. You'll face challenges but enjoy remarkable growth as you push the boundaries.

### 15 Thursday

Moon ingress Capricorn. You may prioritize practical matters and take a more structured approach to achieving your objectives. The energy of Capricorn encourages you to focus on long-term success. It's a good time for setting goals, planning strategies, and working diligently towards your aspirations. Embrace the grounded nature of Capricorn to make steady progress and create a solid foundation for your future endeavors.

### 16 Friday

A new chapter unfolds, emphasizing a shift to a more social environment. It's a carefree and joyous period that allows you to relax and unwind with friends. Networking within your community brings opportunities for collaboration, fostering the development of your creative talents. Embracing your gifts leads to an expansive chapter, cultivating growth in various aspects of your life and infusing it with happiness.

### 17 Saturday

When the Sun aligns with Uranus, you may experience electrifying energy and a strong urge for change and individuality. This cosmic conjunction brings a sense of innovation and rebellion, inspiring you to break free from limitations and embrace your unique self-expression. You might feel an intensified need for independence and a desire to challenge conventional norms. It is a time to embrace authenticity, explore possibilities, and step out of your comfort zone.

### 18 Sunday

When Mercury squares Mars, it can bring a heightened sense of mental energy and a tendency towards impulsive or heated communication. Thoughts and ideas may come rapidly, but there can also be a risk of conflicts arising from hasty words or impatience. It's essential to be mindful of comments and actions during this time, as there is a potential for misunderstandings. The Moon's ingress into Aquarius adds a touch of intellectual detachment and innovation to the mix.

### 19 Monday

The possibilities this week are accompanied by a lighter energy surrounding your social life. This highly productive phase encourages socialization and networking, providing you with increased stability and improved building blocks in your life. Engaging discussions nurture enterprising ideas, creating exciting potential for collaborations. You'll enjoy a more prosperous life experience as you partake in fun and engaging activities with friends.

### 20 Tuesday

When the Sun forms a sextile aspect with Saturn, it brings a harmonious blend of stability and ambition. This aspect enhances your focus, discipline, and ability to plan for the future. It encourages you to take practical steps towards your goals and work diligently towards achieving them. You may feel more organized and structured in your approach, allowing you to make steady progress. With the Moon entering Pisces, your emotions may become more intuitive and sensitive.

### 21 Wednesday

You benefit from the upcoming events that are primed to propel your dreams and growth journey. These opportunities serve as an exciting sign that life is shifting in your favor. By navigating through the changing environment with agility and adaptability, you'll establish a stable foundation for your life. Please focus on the areas that hold the most significance, as they lead to thriving and prospering. This period highlights a social aspect that fosters engaging group interactions.

### 22 Thursday

The Sun's sextile aspect to Neptune enhances intuition, creativity, and spiritual awareness. With the Moon entering Aries, there is a surge of fiery energy and a desire for new beginnings. You may feel renewed motivation, independence, and willingness to take initiative in pursuing your goals. It's a time to embrace your inner warrior and fearlessly embark on new adventures. Trust your instincts and follow your passions as you navigate this dynamic and transformative energy.

### 23 Friday

Embrace new possibilities as they bring goodness into your life. Despite the significant challenges you've faced, you're emerging more resilient and prepared for the transformative cycle ahead. The arrival of new information enables you to shift gears and explore new areas that fully utilize your talents. This growth-oriented phase elevates your skills, lays solid foundations, and expands your world.

### 24 Saturday

Moon enters Taurus, bringing stability, grounding, and a desire for comfort and security. With Mercury conjunct with Uranus, your mind fills with innovative ideas. This aspect stimulates your intellect and encourages you to think outside the box. You may experience sudden insights and flashes of inspiration, propelling you to explore new and unconventional paths of communication and learning. It's a time to embrace your unique perspective and the power of your thoughts.

### 25 Sunday

Saturn ingress Aries is a time for personal growth and self-improvement, where you may need to confront and overcome any tendencies towards impatience or impulsiveness. Saturn in Aries encourages you to cultivate patience, endurance, and resilience as you navigate the various areas of your life. It's an opportunity to establish a solid foundation for your endeavors and build a strong personal responsibility.

### 26 Monday

Mercury ingress Gemini transit enhances your ability to express yourself clearly and effectively, making it an ideal time for engaging in meaningful conversations. Mercury sextile Saturn supports you in bringing structure to your communication. This alignment helps you think critically, plan strategically, and articulate your ideas. With the Moon also moving into Gemini, emotions align with your mental energy, creating a balance between thoughts and feelings.

### 27 Tuesday

During the New Moon, you can start fresh and set new intentions. It's a powerful time for personal transformation and deep introspection. Mercury trine Pluto infuses your thoughts and communication with intensity and depth. You can uncover hidden truths and penetrate the core of any matter. This aspect empowers you to express yourself confidently and engage in profound conversations. It's a time of heightened mental understanding and strategic thinking.

### 28 Wednesday

As the Moon moves into Cancer, you may feel a deep emotional connection and nurturing energy. This ingress invites you to turn your attention inward and focus on your emotional well-being. You might seek comfort and security in familiar environments or connect with loved ones who provide emotional support. Your intuition is heightened during this time, allowing you to tune into your needs and those around you.

### 29 Thursday

A healing influence envelops your current situation, providing a more robust foundation that promotes balance and growth. You'll find it to be spiritually rejuvenating, helping to heal old wounds. The enticing options that lie ahead enable you to move away from sorrow, making room for a rewarding and harmonious phase in your life. Prioritizing your social connections introduces a winning chapter.

# JUNE

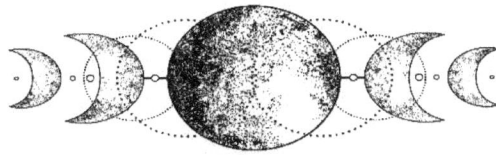

MOON MAGIC

| Sun | Mon | Tue | Wed | Thu | Fri | Sat |
|-----|-----|-----|-----|-----|-----|-----|
| 1 | 2 | 3 | 4 | 5 | 6 | 7 |
| 8 | 9 | 10 | 11 | 12 | 13 | 14 |
| 15 | 16 | 17 | 18 | 19 | 20 | 21 |
| 22 | 23 | 24 | 25 | 26 | 27 | 28 |
| 29 | 30 | | | | | |

# New Moon

# STRAWBERRY MOON

**30 Friday**

As the Sun aligns with Mercury, your mind illuminates with clarity and confidence. You possess a heightened ability to express yourself with authenticity and assertiveness. This harmonious conjunction empowers you to confidently communicate your ideas and thoughts, making it a good time for meaningful conversations and negotiations. Meanwhile, with the Moon entering Leo, your emotions are infused with passion and creativity.

**31 Saturday**

Amid a transitional phase that may feel unsettling, remember to focus on nurturing the foundations that hold significance in your life. It prepares you for a bustling period that helps you gather your resources and embark on a new and exciting chapter filled with potential. News on the horizon delivers heartwarming information, giving you a considerable boost and a hint of a unique journey ahead. Your transition to a favorable cycle elevates your vision for future growth.

**1 Sunday**

Attractive options lead you away from sorrow, opening the door to a more active social life. This socializing opportunity provides the perfect backdrop for expanding your horizons and meeting new friends. The forthcoming environment promotes lively discussions, pushing the boundaries, and growing life. A new friendship comes to light, offering opportunities to engage with someone who piques your curiosity and interest.

**2 Monday**

As the Moon moves into Virgo, you may become more focused on the details and seek practical solutions in your daily life. Use your keen eye to identify areas of improvement in various aspects of your life, whether it's your work, health, or relationships. Take the opportunity to make minor, practical adjustments that can lead to greater efficiency and productivity. Embrace the grounding energy of Virgo, and let it guide you in refining your daily habits.

**3 Tuesday**

Positive news emerges shattering barriers that hinder your best achievements. Your unique identity and willingness to embrace novelty attract a pleasing outcome. Expanding your horizons takes on a fresh approach, signaling a fortunate turn in your life. A lucky break materializes, paving the way for the realization of a long-held dream. This promising development propels you toward nurturing your goals with newfound enthusiasm.

**4 Wednesday**

As the Moon enters Libra, you may feel harmony and a desire for balance as it is a time to focus on your relationships and seek to establish a sense of equilibrium in your interactions. You may find yourself naturally drawn to social activities and pursuing opportunities for collaboration and cooperation. Your diplomatic skills and ability to see multiple perspectives can be valuable assets during this phase as you strive to maintain peace and fairness in your connections.

**5 Thursday**

Venus sextile Jupiter aspect brings opportunities for growth, abundance, and positive experiences in your relationships, creativity, and overall well-being. You may feel a sense of optimism and a desire to connect with others, fostering love, joy, and harmony. It's a time to embrace the beauty and pleasures of life and cultivate a mindset of abundance and gratitude. Additionally, with Mercury sextile Mars, you can effectively express your thoughts and ideas.

## 6 Friday

Venus ingress Taurus is a good time for cultivating self-worth, nurturing existing relationships, and attracting new ones based on shared values and mutual admiration. You may feel a more profound need for security and stability, both emotionally and materially. Take the time to indulge in self-care, pampering, and enjoying the physical world. Use this period to savor the beauty of life and create an environment that nourishes your senses and brings you peace and harmony.

## 7 Saturday

Moon ingress Scorpio's an influential period for personal growth and healing as you confront and release any emotional baggage or patterns that no longer serve you. Trust your instincts and intuition, as they will guide you towards a greater understanding of yourself and others. Embrace the transformative power of this lunar transit and allow it to lead you on a journey of emotional renewal and empowerment.

## 8 Sunday

When Mercury conjuncts Jupiter, you can expect a boost in your mental abilities and a surge of expansive and optimistic thinking. Your mind becomes sharper and more receptive to new ideas and possibilities. This conjunction enhances your communication skills, making it a time to broaden your horizons and explore different perspectives. Mercury's ingress into Cancer makes your thoughts and communication more emotional.

**9 Monday**

When Mercury squares Saturn, it can bring some challenges to thought processes. You may feel restricted or limited in expressing yourself or finding the right words. However, it's important to remember that this is just a temporary aspect, and with patience, you can overcome any communication difficulties. As the Moon ingresses into Sagittarius, it brings a sense of expansion to your emotions. You may desire freedom and exploration, seeking new perspectives.

**10 Tuesday**

Anticipate a change of pace as an invitation to mingle surfaces, injecting fresh potential into your social life. Exciting news becomes the catalyst for stepping up and sharing experiences with friends. Manifesting happiness takes center stage, and a lighter, more joyful approach guides you toward sunny skies. Quality time spent with valued companions sets the tone for a supportive journey marked by thoughtful communication and abundance.

**11 Wednesday**

During a Full Moon, the lunar energy peaks, illuminating areas of your life that are ready for release or culmination. It's a time of heightened emotions and increased awareness. As the Moon shines, it invites you to reflect on your feelings, relationships, and desires. Mercury and Venus's harmonious aspect brings a sense of ease and grace to your communication and social interactions in this phase.

**12 Thursday**

The disciplined nature of Capricorn helps you stay focused and determined, allowing you to make progress in your endeavors. You may find yourself drawn to tasks that require patience and perseverance as you understand the importance of laying a solid foundation for your future. Use this time to organize your life, set realistic targets, and prioritize your commitments. With the Moon in Capricorn, you can channel your emotions into productive action and achieve success.

### 13 Friday

News unfolds, revealing a captivating dimension that piques your curiosity and sparks a desire for deeper exploration. This newfound area injects a delightful social element, infusing your life with joy and excitement shared among friends as you dedicate ample time to broaden your horizons. A path of engaging possibilities materializes, propelling you toward a vibrant and enriching chapter. Nurturing your extended social connections fosters well-being and happiness.

### 14 Saturday

When the Moon enters Aquarius, you may experience a shift in your emotional energy. Aquarius brings a sense of independence, innovation, and intellectual curiosity to your emotions. You may crave intellectual stimulation, seek new perspectives, and engage in meaningful conversations during this time. You may also feel a more substantial social consciousness and a desire to contribute to causes promoting progress and change.

### 15 Sunday

When Mars squares Uranus and Jupiter squares Saturn, you may experience a clash between your desire for freedom and the need for stability and responsibility. It can create a sense of tension and unpredictability in your life. You may feel the urge to break free from limitations and take risks, but at the same time, you recognize the importance of maintaining structure and discipline. It's a balancing act between asserting your independence and adhering to practical constraints.

### 16 Monday

Moon ingress Pisces. Pisces is a compassionate sign, inviting you to connect with your inner world and explore the depths of your feelings. During this time, you may experience heightened empathy and a greater awareness of the energies around you. It's a time to trust your instincts and tap into your imagination and creativity. Allow yourself to dream, express your emotions, and seek solace in activities that nourish your soul.

### 17 Tuesday

When Mars ingresses Virgo, you are motivated to dive into practical tasks and focus on the details of your daily life. Virgo is an analytical and diligent sign, urging you to refine skills, organize your environment, and pursue self-improvement. During this period, you may feel a surge of energy to tackle projects, establish routines, and enhance efficiency. Your attention to detail and desire for orderliness can bring a sense of accomplishment as you strive for perfection in your endeavors.

### 18 Wednesday

When the Moon ingress Aries, you feel a surge of energy and assertiveness. Aries is a fire sign known for its boldness, courage, and initiative. You may take charge, pursue your passions, and embrace new beginnings during this time. Your enthusiasm and drive heighten, motivating you to take action and go after what you want. It's a time for self-discovery, personal growth, and embracing your individuality.

### 19 Thursday

You may grapple with conflicting desires and ideals when Jupiter forms a square with Neptune. Jupiter represents expansion, growth, and optimism, while Neptune embodies dreams, spirituality, and illusions. This aspect can create tension between your aspirations and the reality of the situation. It's essential to be cautious of over-idealizing or being overly optimistic without grounding your plans in practicality.

**20 Friday**

Your creative energy soars, connecting you with profound epiphanies and insights into the path ahead. Fresh opportunities beckon, offering the chance to develop novel facets in your life. Surprises on the horizon tempt you to explore uncharted territories, keeping your energy open and poised to secure new opportunities as they present themselves. Your creativity stays ablaze as you juggle multiple prospects.

**21 Saturday**

As the Moon enters Taurus and the Sun moves into Cancer during the June Solstice, you may feel a profound energy shift. Taurus brings a sense of stability, grounding, and connection to the material world. It encourages you to focus on the practical aspects of life and find comfort in familiar surroundings. Meanwhile, Cancer's influence fosters a deeper emotional connection and enables you to nurture yourself and those around you.

**22 Sunday**

With Mars forming a harmonious sextile to Jupiter and the Sun in a challenging square aspect to Saturn, you find yourself in a dynamic and potentially transformative phase. The Mars-Jupiter sextile amplifies your drive for growth and expansion. It encourages you to take bold actions, embrace opportunities, and pursue your ambitions enthusiastically. However, the Sun-Saturn square may present obstacles or limitations that test your resilience and determination.

### 23 Monday

Moon ingress Gemini. Sun square Neptune. Trust your intuition and rely on your inner wisdom to make sound decisions. By embracing a flexible mindset and maintaining a healthy balance between imagination and practicality, you can navigate this transit with grace and adaptability, allowing the magic of the Moon in Gemini to inspire your intellectual pursuits and interpersonal connections. Maintain clarity and ensure actions align with your true intentions and values.

### 24 Tuesday

Sun conjunct Jupiter. You have the potential to achieve great things and make significant progress in your personal and professional endeavors. Embrace the positive energy and take bold steps forward, knowing that the universe supports your journey toward fulfillment and achievement. Trust in your abilities and remain open to the blessings and opportunities that come your way. Your self-belief and optimism will pave the way for a brighter and more expansive future.

### 25 Wednesday

With the Moon entering Cancer and marking the arrival of a New Moon, you reveal a potent opportunity for emotional renewal and fresh beginnings. The energy of the Cancer Moon nurtures your dynamic landscape, encouraging you to connect with your innermost feelings and desires. This New Moon phase invites you to set intentions and plant the seeds of your aspirations, symbolizing a time of growth and manifestation.

### 26 Thursday

With Mercury forming a harmonious sextile aspect with Uranus and the Sun forming a sextile with Mars, electric and dynamic energy surrounds you. These aspects encourage you to embrace your unique ideas and express yourself with confidence and passion. The ingress of Mercury into Leo amplifies your communication skills and enables you to think creatively and think outside the box.

### 27 Friday

Moon ingress Leo lunar transit invites you to embrace joy, playfulness, and a sense of self-assuredness. Embrace your individuality, celebrate your strengths, and let your inner fire ignite your pursuits. Embody the energy of the confident and charismatic Leo as you embark on this lunar phase, and let it inspire you to pursue your passions with passion and enthusiasm. Let the Moon in Leo guide you towards embracing your true self and living purposefully and authentically.

### 28 Saturday

The new possibilities ahead are accompanied by a lighter energy surrounding your social life. This highly productive phase encourages socialization and networking, providing you with increased stability and improved building blocks in your life. Engaging discussions nurture enterprising ideas, creating exciting potential for collaborations. You'll enjoy a more prosperous life experience as you partake in fun and engaging activities with friends.

### 29 Sunday

Your journey includes many valuable gifts to share, particularly when it comes to developing your talents. As you get more involved in honing your skills, unique abilities emerge, offering you ample room for expansion. Your willingness to invest in your abilities sets you on a trajectory of success, elevating various aspects of your life and instilling you with a deep sense of optimism. You'll face significant challenges and enjoy remarkable growth as you push the boundaries.

# JULY

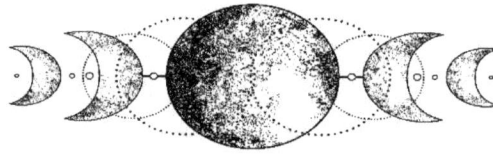

MOON MAGIC

| Sun | Mon | Tue | Wed | Thu | Fri | Sat |
|-----|-----|-----|-----|-----|-----|-----|
|     |     | 1   | 2   | 3   | 4   | 5   |
| 6   | 7   | 8   | 9   | 10  | 11  | 12  |
| 13  | 14  | 15  | 16  | 17  | 18  | 19  |
| 20  | 21  | 22  | 23  | 24  | 25  | 26  |
| 27  | 28  | 29  | 30  | 31  |     |     |

VIRGO

# New Moon

# BUCK MOON

**30 Monday**

Embrace improvement as new information ushers in a busy and productive phase, propelling you toward the realization of your goals. Imminent rising prospects stir the essence of manifestation, enabling your talents to flourish and guide you toward a venture that promises advancement. Infuse ambition into your endeavors to achieve a golden outcome. Under the positive influence, new goals take shape, bringing about a pleasing and fulfilling result.

**1 Tuesday**

Moon ingress Libra is a time to build connections, foster harmony, and cultivate a sense of beauty and aesthetic appreciation in your surroundings. You may find yourself drawn to social activities, seeking the company of others, and engaging in meaningful conversations. The Libra Moon encourages you to consider different perspectives and find common ground. Use this time to nurture your relationships, express your creativity, and find ways to bring balance into life.

**2 Wednesday**

A refreshing change of pace unveils new information. Embracing openness to novel options sparks inspiration, facilitating functional changes that enhance your capabilities and promote the refinement of your skills. Engage in a bustling time of crafting your vision, expanding life outward, and gaining traction on growth. The emphasis on advancement promises a pleasing result, leading to a goal-oriented chapter that propels you toward success in your professional journey.

**3 Thursday**

Life unfolds with glittering possibilities encouraging expansion, guiding you toward a progressive and prosperous journey that nurtures your creative abilities. Collaborating with your skills brings assignments aligning you with growth. The wheels move away from outworn areas, favoring expansion as life progresses towards an enriching period of developing unique goals. Reevaluating marks a turning point, refueling energy tanks and propelling you to set inspiring goals.

### 4 Friday

With Venus conjunct Uranus and entering Gemini, unexpected shifts and exciting encounters may arise. This planetary alignment encourages you to embrace spontaneity and explore new connections that bring freedom and excitement. Simultaneously, as Neptune turns retrograde, you are called to reevaluate your dreams, illusions, and spiritual pursuits. It's a time to reflect on the boundaries between reality and fantasy and to gain clarity on your higher aspirations.

### 5 Saturday

Prioritizing yourself becomes the cornerstone for cultivating peace in your immediate environment. Establishing boundaries with toxic influences proves beneficial for your well-being, propelling you toward a pivotal step in the development of your romantic life. This shift opens the door to a unique chapter that rekindles potential. You deepen connections through thoughtful conversations that usher in harmony, creating ideal conditions for advancement.

### 6 Sunday

When Venus forms a sextile aspect with Saturn, you may find stability and harmony in your relationships and creative endeavors. This transit encourages you to build solid foundations and cultivate lasting connections based on trust and mutual support. It's a favorable time to establish boundaries and make practical decisions contributing to long-term growth. And as Venus sextiles Neptune, dreamy and romantic energy permeates your experiences.

**7 Monday**

When Uranus enters Gemini, it brings innovation and intellectual curiosity into your life. This transit encourages you to embrace change, explore new ideas, and adopt a more progressive mindset. You may draw unconventional relationships and creative endeavors challenging the status quo. Meanwhile, Venus forming a trine with Pluto deepens your emotional connections and intensifies your passions.

**8 Tuesday**

Pushing back barriers becomes vital in asserting yourself and pursuing dreams, laying the groundwork for improvement, and initiating a new growth cycle. Expanding opportunities blaze a trail forward toward rising prospects, presenting a positive trend as life picks up momentum. Amidst change, a journey capturing the essence of luck emerges, cultivating new options and breaking up stagnant patterns as you elevate your skills to the next level.

**9 Wednesday**

Moon ingress Capricorn. You may feel a greater need for structure, organization, and stability in your personal and professional life. Embrace this energy by setting clear intentions, establishing a solid plan, and taking practical actions toward your desired outcomes. The power of Capricorn supports your ability to plan, organize, and make progress in areas that are important to you. Remember to balance work and rest, as self-care and rejuvenation are equally crucial for success.

**10 Thursday**

The Full Moon is a powerful time to release what no longer serves you and let go of any emotional baggage. The Full Moon illuminates the path ahead, providing clarity and insight into your desires and intentions. Use this time to connect with your inner self, trust your intuition, and set personal growth and manifestation intentions. Embrace the transformative energy of the Full Moon and allow it to guide you on your journey toward self-discovery and fulfillment.

### 11 Friday

Moon ingress Aquarius. Embrace the freedom to express your true self and let your authenticity shine. It is a time to break free from convention and embrace your independent spirit. Trust in your intuition and allow your mind to expand as you explore new possibilities and forge connections with others who inspire you. Let the energy of Aquarius guide you in embracing your brilliance and positively impacting the world around you.

### 12 Saturday

The expansion of your social sphere not only broadens horizons but initiates a vital transition that nurtures companionship and attracts positive energies into your life. Immersing yourself in a social environment helps balance foundations, with communication and shared activities nourishing your soul. New possibilities abound, allowing you to strike gold by actively engaging in your social life, smoothing over life's rough edges, and fostering companionship.

### 13 Sunday

Saturn turns retrograde. With the Moon's ingress into Pisces, you are encouraged to tap into your intuition and emotional sensitivity. Trust your inner guidance and explore imagination, creativity, and spirituality. Embrace the fluid and intuitive nature of Pisces as you navigate the transformative energies of Saturn's retrograde. It is a time for deep inner work, healing, and spiritual growth as you uncover the wisdom and strength within you.

### 14 Monday

Innovating and adapting becomes your key to breaking through barriers and paving the way for rising prospects in various aspects of your life. An extended period of chasing dreams and exploring new pathways emerges, offering fertile ground for growth. Trusting your instincts propels you forward, aligning your decisions with a unique direction that Serendipity lights up, bringing forth an uptick of exciting possibilities.

### 15 Tuesday

Good news flows into your life, laying the groundwork for improved security. Focusing on advancing your vision for future growth facilitates essential changes, offering rising prospects in your working life. Your willingness to explore leads to a positive result, opening the gateway toward growth. Soon, you find yourself busy developing skills and navigating the path ahead. A refreshing shift unfolds when exciting news surfaces, providing a viable option for progress.

### 16 Wednesday

When the Moon enters Aries, you may feel a surge of energy and assertiveness. It's a time of new beginnings and taking action. Your emotions are fiery and passionate, fueling your drive and motivation. You have a strong desire to pursue your goals and make things happen. This transit is the perfect time to embrace your inner warrior and confidently tackle challenges. Trust your instincts and take bold steps forward.

### 17 Thursday

Moving towards greener pastures helps you escape limiting situations, offering a time of growth and new possibilities. Information arriving as a game-changer unveils new opportunities, motivating you to push past limitations and explore exciting new options. Being receptive to change rejuvenates and re-energizes your spirit, guiding you toward a journey that promotes wellness and harmony. A vibrant time for nurturing foundations and developing goals is on the horizon.

## 18 Friday

When Mercury turns retrograde, you may notice a shift in communication and travel plans. It's a time to slow down and reflect on your thoughts and words. Please take the opportunity to review and revise any essential documents or agreements before finalizing them. With the Moon moving into Taurus, you're encouraged to ground yourself and focus on the practical aspects of life. It's a favorable time for stability and reliability.

## 19 Saturday

Creating space for inner reflection becomes a powerful tool to connect with insight and information. Weeding out distractions and nurturing quiet time enables you to hear the wisdom within. The arrival of something tempting breathes fresh air into your surroundings, offering a soothing element that harmonizes your spirit. This joyous shift helps you break free from limiting patterns, guiding you toward an open road ahead as you navigate with ease along unique pathways.

## 20 Sunday

When the Moon moves into Gemini, it shifts your emotional energy. You may feel more curious, adaptable, and inclined to explore various interests and engage in lively conversations. This transit is a time to embrace mental stimulation and social interactions. Your mind is agile, and you have a natural ability to absorb information quickly. It's a favorable period for learning, networking, and exchanging ideas with others.

### 21 Monday

Advancement is on the horizon as you set your sights on achieving your vision and charting a course for career growth. Revealed pathways deepen your knowledge and talents, facilitating a transition towards learning new areas. This positions you to advance your working life to the next level, connecting with a vibrant landscape that fosters growth. Changing priorities initiates a new life cycle, injecting excitement as you expand barriers and head toward growth.

### 22 Tuesday

Moon ingress Cancer. Sun ingress Leo. Allow your emotions to guide you, and trust your intuition as you navigate through this phase. Find joy in connecting with loved ones, creating a warm and supportive environment, and celebrating your strengths and passions. Embrace the powerful combination of Cancer's sensitivity and Leo's confidence to bring forth your authentic essence and make a positive impact in your life and the lives of others.

### 23 Wednesday

Sun sextile Uranus. Venus square Mars. Navigating this energy with awareness, practicing open communication, and finding constructive ways to channel your passions are essential. Embrace the Sun's transformative influence and the Venus-Mars dynamic to embrace your uniqueness, ignite your desires, and make positive changes in your life. Trust yourself and be open to the unexpected opportunities that may come your way.

### 24 Thursday

With the Sun trine Saturn, you infuse with stability, discipline, and practicality. This harmonious aspect empowers you to progress steadily toward goals as you find the perfect balance between ambition and responsibility. The Moon's ingress into Leo further amplifies your self-confidence, creativity, and passion. You are inspired to express authentically and shine your unique light. The New Moon signals a fresh start, a time of setting intentions and planting seeds for the future.

**25 Friday**

Sun opposed Pluto's calls for self-reflection, inner strength, and the willingness to release old patterns or attachments. Embrace the transformative energy of this aspect and allow it to empower you to face your shadows, release what no longer serves your growth, and emerge more robust and authentic in the process. Remember that you have the strength and resilience to navigate any challenges, and this opposition can ultimately lead you to a place of empowerment.

**26 Saturday**

When the Moon ingresses Virgo, you may feel an inclination to focus on practical matters and details in your life. It is when you are likely to have a heightened sense of organization, efficiency, and attention to cleanliness. You may find yourself analyzing and refining your routines, seeking ways to improve productivity and create a sense of order in your daily activities. This influence can also bring a desire for self-improvement and a willingness to work diligently toward goals.

**27 Sunday**

Life unfolds to support your efforts in improving circumstances, reaching a turning point that allows unique possibilities to blossom. Grounded energy balances foundations, reawakening a sense of adventure and ushering in a freedom-loving vibe. Rejuvenation wipes the slate clean, releasing stress and paving the way for a fresh chapter filled with exciting possibilities. Vibrant social bonds and lively discussions become the cornerstone of this positive outcome.

**28 Monday**

Moving forward ushers in a surge of optimism, allowing luck to flow into your life. This creative period immerses you in the development of new journeys, releasing shadows and healing the past. It marks a freedom-driven journey, opening floodgates to unique opportunities. Acting on instincts uncovers refreshing options that promise a bright future. Something special is poised to bloom in your world, expanding the borders and positioning you for growth.

**29 Tuesday**

Moon ingress Libra transit encourages you to seek peace and understanding in your relationships, and you may find yourself more willing to compromise and cooperate with those around you. Your focus might shift towards creating a harmonious and aesthetically pleasing environment and seeking out activities that bring joy and enjoyment. You may feel drawn to socializing and engaging in meaningful conversations with friends and loved ones.

**30 Wednesday**

Research and exploration open high-level options, bringing a newfound project that inspires and motivates. Staying flexible and adaptable proves crucial in weathering storms and heading toward advancement. Pushing back barriers improves foundations, and a transformational aspect highlights golden opportunities. Staying open to new possibilities and connecting with innovative individuals draw positive outcomes.

**31 Thursday**

The Sun conjunct Mercury enhances your communicative abilities, allowing you to express your thoughts and ideas clearly and confidently. This alignment supports open and honest conversations, making it an excellent time for heartfelt discussions and sharing your feelings with those you trust. Use this cosmic energy to foster meaningful connections and delve into the depths of your emotions as you embrace the power of vulnerability and authenticity in your interactions.

# AUGUST

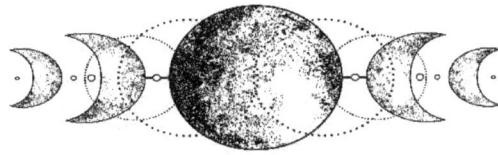

MOON MAGIC

| Sun | Mon | Tue | Wed | Thu | Fri | Sat |
|-----|-----|-----|-----|-----|-----|-----|
|     |     |     |     |     | 1   | 2   |
| 3   | 4   | 5   | 6   | 7   | 8   | 9   |
| 10  | 11  | 12  | 13  | 14  | 15  | 16  |
| 17  | 18  | 19  | 20  | 21  | 22  | 23  |
| 24  | 25  | 26  | 27  | 28  | 29  | 30  |
| 31  |     |     |     |     |     |     |

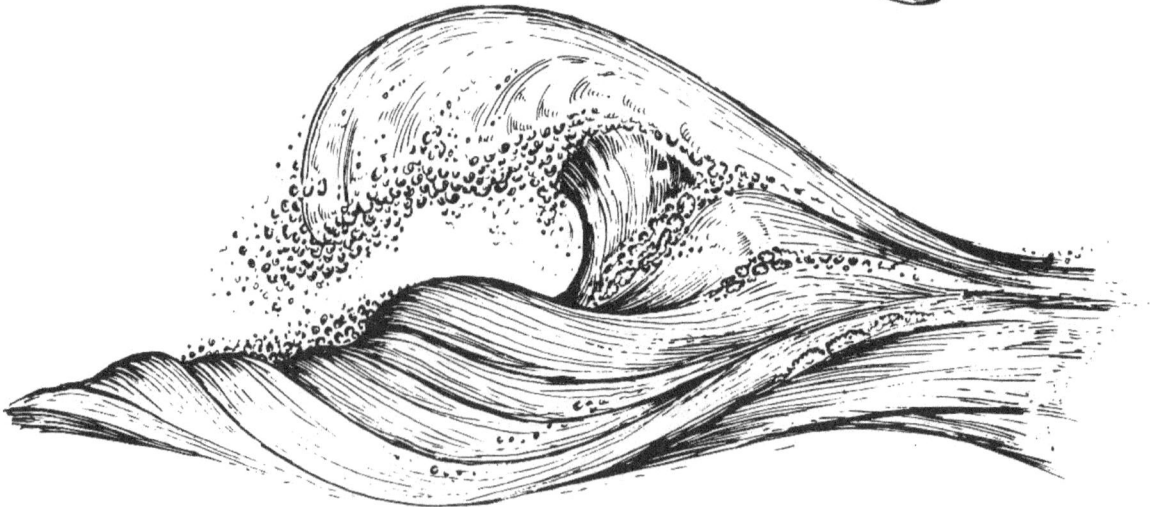

# NEW MOON

# STURGEON MOON

### 1 Friday

With Venus forming a square aspect to Saturn, you may encounter some challenges in your relationships and experience a sense of restriction or limitation in expressing your affections. This aspect can bring forth feelings of insecurity or doubts about the viability of your connections with others. You might find it challenging to feel fully appreciated or valued in your relationships, leading to moments of self-doubt or questioning your worth.

### 2 Saturday

Life lends support to your efforts by enhancing foundations and drawing lighter energy that nourishes well-being and renewal. Expressive and expansive times rule spontaneous get-togethers and mingling, linking up with a forward shift encouraging personal growth and future planning. Lively discussions bring insightful ideas to light, emphasizing the positive energy in your life and offering a platform for shared wisdom.

### 3 Sunday

Moon ingress Sagittarius is a favorable time to engage in activities that challenge your intellect and provide opportunities for personal growth. Embrace the spirit of spontaneity and open-mindedness, as the energy of Sagittarius encourages you to venture into new territories and discover exciting possibilities. Trust your intuition and let the optimistic vibes guide you toward exciting opportunities for learning and exploration.

## 4 Monday

Turning the corner, you strike gold and chart a course towards growth, entering an extended time that reinvents the potential in your world. A transformational aspect has a profound effect on your spirit, offering healing and well-being as you improve foundations and nurture possibilities. Pushing barriers back and embracing change, a new area inspires excitement, and conditions for growth ripen, bringing stability and progression.

## 5 Tuesday

As the Moon moves into Capricorn, you may feel a shift towards a more grounded and practical approach to your emotions. This transit encourages you to focus on your long-term goals and responsibilities and to take a disciplined and structured approach to your emotional well-being. You might find yourself more determined to succeed and progress personally and professionally. Embrace the energy of this transit to build a solid foundation for your emotional growth and stability.

## 6 Wednesday

As Mars moves into Libra, you might experience a shift in your energy and approach to relationships. Your desire for justice and fairness heightens, and you may feel more inclined to stand up for the rights of others. Use this energy to foster cooperation and build stronger connections with those around you. Remember that finding a middle ground and maintaining a sense of equilibrium can lead to positive outcomes during this Mars in Libra period.

## 7 Thursday

Opportunities ahead introduce a newfound endeavor inspiring motivation, creativity, and growth. Banishing cobwebs, you enter a time of progress and rising prospects, shining a light on using your talents to expand your life. Researching, learning, and growing a remarkable area sets the stage for a vibrant landscape of possibilities, initiating a new phase that revolutionizes the potential in your world. Life becomes groovy as you navigate a time ripe with remarkable possibilities.

### 8 Friday

With the Moon moving into Aquarius and Mars forming a trine with Uranus, you may feel the excitement and a desire for change and innovation. You are more open to exploring new ideas and unconventional approaches to challenges. Your energy electrifies, and you may be motivated to take risks and break free from old patterns or routines. This cosmic combination encourages you to embrace your individuality and be open to unexpected opportunities that come your way.

### 9 Saturday

You might grapple with conflicting energies and emotions, with Mars forming oppositions to Saturn and Neptune and a Full Moon in the mix. The Mars-Saturn opposition could create a sense of frustration or obstacles, making it challenging to move forward with your plans. You might feel you face limitations or responsibilities demanding your attention and patience. The Full Moon amplifies emotions, bringing issues to the surface and intensifying your feelings.

### 10 Sunday

With the Moon entering Pisces and Mars forming a trine with Pluto, you might experience a blend of intuition and personal power. Emotions may heighten, and you might seek deeper introspection and spiritual exploration. Allow yourself to connect with your inner world, and trust your instincts as they can guide you towards transformative experiences. The harmonious trine between Mars and Pluto empowers you to tackle challenges with determination and resilience.

### 11 Monday

As Mercury turns direct, you can expect relief and clarity in your communication and thought processes. Any delays or misunderstandings that might have occurred during its retrograde phase will start clearing up, allowing you to move forward more confidently and decisively. It is an excellent time to tackle pending tasks, make important decisions, and communicate your ideas effectively. Remember to stay flexible; the post-retrograde period can bring insights and opportunities.

### 12 Tuesday

The Venus conjunct Jupiter aspect brings optimism, joy, and abundance to your relationships and experiences. As the Moon enters Aries, you'll likely feel a boost of energy and enthusiasm, motivating you to take action and pursue your passions. This combination of celestial events creates an atmosphere of positive change, expansion, and self-assurance, urging you to make the most of the opportunities that come your way and embrace a sense of adventure and growth.

### 13 Wednesday

In a time of transformation, reflection and contemplation become valuable tools to nurture stability and balance. Pulling back from extra demands and focusing on building blocks promotes harmony, putting you in the direction that offers growth and progress. This time is for developing goals, increasing wellness, and enjoying pleasurable pastimes. This journey brings insights into the path ahead, evaluating all aspects of life for renewal and rejuvenation.

### 14 Thursday

As the Moon enters Taurus, you might notice a shift towards a more grounded and stable emotional state. This transit encourages you to seek comfort, security, and simplicity in your surroundings. You may find yourself drawn to activities that promote relaxation and pleasure, such as enjoying good food, spending time in nature, or indulging in creative pursuits. It is an excellent time to focus on self-care and nurturing yourself physically and emotionally.

**15 Friday**

With Mercury sextile Mars, you may experience a boost in mental energy and a heightened ability to communicate effectively. Your thoughts and ideas are sharp and clear, and you can articulate them with passion and confidence. It encourages you to act on your plans and ideas, as your mind and communication align with your assertiveness. It's a favorable time to engage in debates, negotiations, or any activity that requires passion and quick thinking.

**16 Saturday**

With the Moon ingress Gemini, you might experience a shift in your emotional state and communication style. This astrological event encourages you to be more curious, adaptable, and friendly. Your mind becomes more active and interested, seeking new information and experiences. You may be open to conversations and eager to engage with others. It is an excellent time to connect with friends, join group activities, or participate in discussions.

**17 Sunday**

A great time unfolds for nurturing your life and establishing new foundations that ignite the fires of your imagination. Vast potential surrounds the periphery of your life, and exploring new options creates forward momentum for developing goals efficiently. Riding a wave of promising energy opens the floodgates to rising potential, allowing you to explore pursuits that offer excellence and progress. A design you hatch gathers pace, landing you in an environment worth your time.

### 18 Monday

When Mercury forms a sextile aspect with Mars, your thoughts and ideas become more dynamic, enabling you to express yourself with confidence and precision. Simultaneously, the Moon's ingress into Cancer brings emotional sensitivity, encouraging you to be nurturing and compassionate towards others. This alignment enhances your ability to connect with people more profoundly, fostering a supportive and empathetic atmosphere.

### 19 Tuesday

Streamlining and refining goals enable you to head towards growth, clearing blocks to establish stable foundations for a thriving chapter ahead. It promotes a time of expansion and opportunity. Positive news brings a refreshing path, nurturing dreams as you evolve and grow on your forward journey. An experimental flavor rekindles vitality, motivating you to tackle new projects. Being open to possibilities helps transition towards rising prospects.

### 20 Wednesday

Moon ingress Leo. You might channel energy into endeavors that align with your passions. It's a great time to engage in activities that bring you joy and allow you to showcase your talents. Remember to balance this self-assuredness with generosity and kindness towards others, as Leo Moon also encourages a warm and caring approach to those around you. Let your inner light illuminate your path and inspire those you encounter.

### 21 Thursday

Your working with your talents releases outworn areas, building stable foundations that rejuvenate your life and translate into a fresh start with rising prospects. Exploring pathways and upgrading your life becomes a focus, leading to the development of career options and the growth of skills. Advancement becomes a tangible outcome as you grow in a transformative journey. Entering a growth cycle allows you to move toward unique opportunities.

## 22 Friday

As the Sun enters Virgo, you might notice a shift in your focus and approach to life. This astrological event encourages you to pay more attention to the details and take a practical and analytical approach to your daily activities. You may feel a stronger sense of responsibility and a desire to organize your surroundings and routines. This transit is an excellent time to set goals, prioritize tasks, and work diligently towards achieving them.

## 23 Saturday

It's a great moment to declutter and create a more harmonious living or working space. As the Moon aligns with the Sun during the New Moon, you can tap into the Virgo energy to set clear and achievable goals, bringing a sense of purpose and direction to your endeavors. Allow this lunar phase to inspire you to be more attentive to your physical and emotional well-being, enabling you to make positive changes and embrace a more balanced and fulfilling life.

## 24 Sunday

With the Sun forming a square aspect with Uranus, you might experience a sense of restlessness and a desire for change. This astrological influence can bring unexpected disruptions and a need to break from routines and limitations. You may crave unconventional ideas or explore new, innovative paths. While this can be an exciting time of experimentation and self-discovery, it's essential to remain adaptable and open-minded, as sudden shifts can challenge your sense of stability.

### 25 Monday

With the Moon's ingress into Libra, you may feel a stronger inclination towards seeking harmony and balance in your emotional life. This astrological influence encourages you to foster greater cooperation and compromise in your relationships, valuing fairness and understanding in your interactions. Additionally, as Venus moves into Leo, your approach to love becomes more vibrant and expressive. Your romantic pursuits could take on a passionate flair.

### 26 Tuesday

The sextile to Uranus adds a touch of excitement and spontaneity, encouraging you to embrace unique and unconventional expressions of affection. This cosmic combination sparks inspiration and originality in your creative endeavors, making it an ideal time to explore new artistic avenues or innovative solutions. The trine to Neptune enhances your sense of empathy and compassion, promoting a deeper understanding and connection with others on a spiritual level.

### 27 Wednesday

Venus opposed Pluto's astrological aspect, which can bring deep-seated issues and hidden desires that demand attention and resolution. You might feel compelled to confront the problems in your interactions, which could lead to challenging dynamics. It's essential to be mindful of power imbalances and manipulative tendencies during this time. Use this opposition as an opportunity for growth and transformation, as it can reveal underlying patterns that need healing and release.

### 28 Thursday

Moon ingress Scorpio. Allow yourself to embrace this transformative influence and use it as an opportunity for self-discovery and personal growth. It's a favorable time to engage in activities that promote healing and emotional release and connect with others on a deeper, more meaningful level. Embrace the Scorpio Moon's passionate and probing nature to gain insights that can lead to greater emotional empowerment and renewal.

**29 Friday**

Uranus sextile Neptune astrological alignment encourages you to think outside the box and explore new possibilities with an open mind. Your imagination sparks, leading to innovative ideas and a deeper understanding of the interconnectedness of all things. During this time, you might feel a stronger urge to break free from limiting beliefs and embrace a more progressive and compassionate outlook on life.

**30 Saturday**

As the Moon enters Sagittarius, you might experience adventurous and optimistic energy. Sagittarius' influence encourages you to embrace a broader perspective and seek knowledge, truth, and new experiences. During this lunar transition, you may find yourself drawn to exploring different cultures, belief systems, or philosophical ideas. Your desire for freedom and expansion heightens, and you may feel a strong urge to break free from routine and embrace spontaneity.

**31 Sunday**

The energy of manifestation brings a vital phase of creativity and renewal, harmonizing with change to bring unique potential into your world and restore foundations. Adapting plays a crucial role in this process. Change surrounds your life, and news arrives to guide you towards developing a journey that grows your talents, launching an exciting endeavor. This creative aspect provides a solid start to increasing your life and advancing your skills in a new area.

# SEPTEMBER

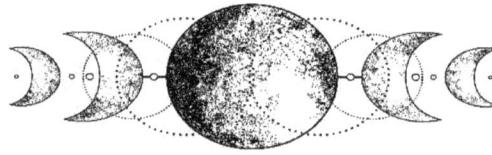

MOON MAGIC

| Sun | Mon | Tue | Wed | Thu | Fri | Sat |
|-----|-----|-----|-----|-----|-----|-----|
|     | 1   | 2   | 3   | 4   | 5   | 6   |
| 7   | 8   | 9   | 10  | 11  | 12  | 13  |
| 14  | 15  | 16  | 17  | 18  | 19  | 20  |
| 21  | 22  | 23  | 24  | 25  | 26  | 27  |
| 28  | 29  | 30  |     |     |     |     |

# NEW MOON

# CORN/HARVEST MOON

**1 Monday**

With Saturn's ingress into Pisces, you may experience a shift in the way you approach responsibilities and boundaries. Pisces' influence can bring a sense of empathy and compassion to your actions, encouraging you to be more understanding and forgiving towards yourself and others. This period might prompt you to reflect on your long-term goals and how you can incorporate more creativity and spirituality into your pursuits.

**2 Tuesday**

Moon ingress Capricorn. Mercury ingress Virgo. This combination of energies fosters a practical and logical mindset, allowing well-informed decisions and effectively articulating your thoughts and ideas. It's a time to set realistic plans and work diligently towards achieving your objectives with an organized approach. Embrace the Capricorn Moon's ambition and the Mercury in Virgo's precision to make the most of this productive and purpose-driven period.

**3 Wednesday**

With Mercury forming a square aspect to Uranus, you might experience a period of mental restlessness and unpredictability. Your thoughts may race, and you could feel a strong urge to break free from routine or conventional thinking. This aspect can bring sudden insight but may also lead to impulsive decisions. It's essential to stay mindful, as the energy of this square can sometimes create misunderstandings or provoke rebellious reactions in interactions with others.

**4 Thursday**

Moon ingress Aquarius is a favorable time to explore innovative ideas and engage in discussions that broaden your understanding of the world. You may also feel a stronger inclination towards humanitarian efforts and supporting causes that resonate with your values. Embrace the progressive and forward-thinking energy of the Aquarius Moon to inspire positive change and foster a sense of camaraderie with others who share your vision for a better future.

### 5 Friday

There is a risk of overestimating your capabilities or being overly optimistic about outcomes, so it's wise to strike a balance between ambition and practicality. Use this powerful combination of Mars and Jupiter to tackle challenges with determination and broaden your horizons, but also remember to pace yourself and avoid unnecessary risks. By being mindful of your actions and decisions, you can make the most of this dynamic energy and achieve progress in your endeavors.

### 6 Saturday

As Uranus turns retrograde, you may experience a shift in the energy of change and innovation. This planetary event prompts you to look inward and reflect on liberating yourself from old patterns and restrictions. It's a time to reassess your desires for independence and embrace the unconventional aspects of your personality. Simultaneously, with the Moon's ingress into Pisces, your emotions become more intuitive and empathetic.

### 7 Sunday

Full Moons often bring emotions to the surface, allowing you to gain deeper insights into your feelings and relationships. It's an opportune moment to let go of what no longer serves you and embrace gratitude for the growth and experiences you've encountered. Take advantage of this lunar phase to meditate, recharge, and set new intentions for the upcoming cycle, harnessing the powerful energy of the Full Moon to guide you on your journey.

**8 Monday**

As the Moon enters Aries, you may feel a surge of energy and renewed enthusiasm. Aries' influence brings a bold and assertive quality to your emotions, making your approach more direct and action-oriented. This transit is a time to be proactive and take the lead in pursuing your goals and desires. You might find yourself eager to tackle challenges head-on and embrace new opportunities with courage and determination.

**9 Tuesday**

Prepare for a seismic shift in your surroundings as upcoming news signals a changing landscape, ushering in a wave of fresh possibilities. These options serve as a wellspring of inspiration, compelling you to push the boundaries of your world. As you ascend the ladder toward new ventures, you unveil the essence of robust and steady progression forged through the crucible of hard work and dedication.

**10 Wednesday**

Moon ingress Taurus. Taurus' influence brings a sense of comfort and a deeper appreciation for the simple pleasures in life. During this lunar transit, you might feel a more substantial need for security and material comforts, seeking to create a harmonious and serene environment for yourself. It is an excellent time to indulge in sensory experiences, such as enjoying delicious food and nature or surrounding yourself with beautiful things.

**11 Thursday**

Your willingness to enhance circumstances propels you toward a journey of promise and progression, fostering life into new areas and flinging open the door to a new chapter. Prosperity in working with talents and growing abilities shapes the path forward into a journey worth developing, drawing growth into your career path through discipline and dedication, marking a period of strategic advancement.

### 12 Friday

With the Sun forming a harmonious sextile to Jupiter, you may feel a surge of optimism and confidence today. This astrological aspect enhances your sense of self-assurance and opens up opportunities for growth and expansion. The Moon's ingress into Gemini adds a touch of curiosity and mental agility, inspiring you to be more adaptable and communicative. You might be eager to engage in conversations and exchange ideas.

### 13 Saturday

It's a favorable time for engaging in conversations, sharing your opinions, and making presentations, as your words carry a sense of authority and authenticity. The conjunction today boosts your intellectual capacity, allowing you to absorb information more readily and see things from a broader perspective. Embrace the powerful synergy of the Sun and Mercury to embrace opportunities for learning, self-expression, and making your voice heard with impact and influence.

### 14 Sunday

Allocate moments within your busy day to pause and reflect, drawing insight and clarity into the path ahead. Trust your instincts as your guide, tapping into inherent wisdom to align yourself with the optimal trajectory for improving your circumstances. Mindfulness and awareness become catalysts for inspiration and heightened creativity, providing a broader perspective on issues blocking progress. This expanded overview empowers you to head for growth.

### 15 Monday

As the Moon moves into Cancer, you may notice a shift in your emotional landscape, with feelings becoming more sensitive and nurturing. Cancer's influence brings a deeper connection to your home and family and a heightened sense of empathy towards others. During this lunar transit, you might seek comfort and security in familiar surroundings, craving emotional closeness with loved ones.

### 16 Tuesday

When Venus forms a sextile aspect with Mars, you may experience a harmonious blending of feminine and masculine energies within you. This astrological alignment brings a sense of balance and mutual attraction between your desires and actions. You might find it easier to express your affections and assert yourself confidently in matters of the heart. This sextile enhances your social charm and magnetism, making you more attractive to others.

### 17 Wednesday

With the Moon moving into Leo, you may feel a surge of confidence and self-expression. This lunar transit encourages you to embrace individuality and seek attention and recognition for your talents and creativity. However, Mercury's opposition to Saturn may introduce a dose of seriousness and caution to your communication style. You might encounter challenges in expressing yourself, as this aspect can bring self-doubt and a tendency to be overly critical of your ideas.

### 18 Thursday

As Mercury enters Libra, you may find yourself seeking more harmony and balance in your communications and thought processes. This astrological shift encourages you to approach discussions with diplomacy and a willingness to see multiple sides of a situation. However, with Mercury opposing Neptune, there could be a tendency for confusion or misunderstandings in your interactions. It's crucial to be cautious of miscommunication or idealizing situations.

**19 Friday**

With Mercury forming trines to Uranus and Pluto, you may experience a period of heightened mental acuity and profound insights. This astrological alignment enhances your ability to think outside the box and embrace innovative ideas. Your mind becomes more open to unconventional approaches, making it an excellent time for problem-solving and creative thinking. The trine to Pluto also brings depth and intensity to your thoughts, allowing you to uncover hidden truths.

**20 Saturday**

When Venus forms a square aspect to Uranus, you may experience a period of unpredictability and excitement in your relationships and desires. This astrological influence can bring sudden changes and unconventional attractions that challenge your sense of stability. You might find yourself drawn to new and unusual experiences, seeking more freedom and independence in your romantic pursuits.

**21 Sunday**

Sun opposed Saturn's astrological aspect, which can bring challenges, making it crucial to approach situations with patience and a realistic outlook. However, as a New Moon graces the sky, you are presented with an opportunity for fresh beginnings and setting intentions for the upcoming lunar cycle. It is an ideal time to let go of any self-doubt or fears that the Sun-Saturn opposition may have stirred within you and embrace renewed determination and perseverance.

**22 Monday**

Mars ingress Scorpio. September Equinox. Sun ingress Libra. It is an excellent time for focusing on relationships and finding ways to create equilibrium in your interactions. With Mars in Scorpio and the Sun in Libra, you may seek transformative experiences and connections while mindful of the need for balance. Embrace this cosmic synergy to embark on a journey of growth and self-discovery, guided by your desire for harmony and understanding.

**23 Tuesday**

Sun opposed Neptune. During this time, you may also find it challenging to set clear boundaries, as Neptune's energy can create a sense of ambiguity and emotional vulnerability. Practicing self-awareness and discernment is crucial to avoid falling into unrealistic expectations or being swayed by external influences. Embrace this time for reflection and inner exploration, using it to gain insight into your dreams and aspirations while remaining grounded in your approach.

**24 Wednesday**

With the Sun forming harmonious trines to Uranus and Pluto, you may experience a period of transformative insights and increased self-awareness. This astrological alignment enhances your ability to embrace change and uniqueness confidently. You might feel inspired to break free from old patterns and seek new growth opportunities. As the Moon moves into Scorpio, your emotions may become more intense and introspective.

**25 Thursday**

Amidst the bustling rhythm of life, a lead worth developing emerges, promising a big reveal that expands your life into new dimensions. This growth, a dynamic force, cranks up the potential in your world, sparking fresh inspiration. You find yourself immersed in an environment that allows you to work with your abilities and promote your skills, creating forward momentum as a pet project opens avenues for talent expression in an exciting arena.

### 26 Friday

As the Moon moves into Sagittarius, you may feel a sense of adventure and a desire for exploration. This lunar transit fosters a spirit of optimism and curiosity, encouraging you to seek new experiences and broaden your horizons. You might find yourself drawn to learning, traveling, or engaging in activities that stimulate your mind and expand your knowledge. The Sagittarius Moon also enhances your enthusiasm and encourages you to embrace a positive outlook on life.

### 27 Saturday

Your life's rich learning and growth paved the way for emerging potentials, possibly leading to the exploration of new hobbies or undiscovered interests. This journey progresses towards meaningful development, spurred by a surprise invitation that sparks a fresh beginning. Tides turn in your favor as curious communication deepens bonds, adding excitement and glamour to your social life and creating an enriching and transformative chapter.

### 28 Sunday

An opportunity to mingle breathes fresh air and sunny skies into your environment, connecting you with friends and companions and unpacking a chapter of social engagement. Nurturing social bonds upgrades your life, sparking curiosity and interest in a situation that inspires you on many levels. Changes resonate warmly, encouraging a greater sense of security and stability as you focus on improving personal bonds.

# OCTOBER

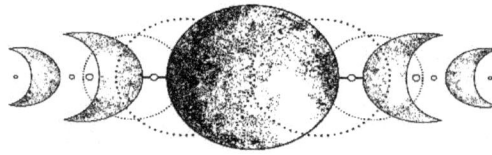

MOON MAGIC

| Sun | Mon | Tue | Wed | Thu | Fri | Sat |
|-----|-----|-----|-----|-----|-----|-----|
|     |     |     | 1   | 2   | 3   | 4   |
| 5   | 6   | 7   | 8   | 9   | 10  | 11  |
| 12  | 13  | 14  | 15  | 16  | 17  | 18  |
| 19  | 20  | 21  | 22  | 23  | 24  | 25  |
| 26  | 27  | 28  | 29  | 30  | 31  |     |

# NEW MOON

# HUNTERS MOON

**29 Monday**

As the Moon enters Capricorn, you may notice a shift towards a more practical and goal-oriented emotional state. This lunar transit fosters a sense of discipline and determination, urging you to focus on your responsibilities and long-term ambitions. Your emotions become more grounded, and you may seek stability and structure. Capricorn's influence encourages you to be productive and take steps towards achieving your objectives.

**30 Tuesday**

Positive news is imminent, illuminating a pathway to change and inspiring impressive results. Staying flexible and adaptable allows you to weather storms and head toward expansion and excitement. Expanding horizons introduces new potential, enabling the building of a balanced foundation focused on developing goals. Your willingness to be open to change sparks remarkable progress, and new options tempt you forward, offering a unique vantage point into view.

**1 Wednesday**

As the Moon moves into Aquarius, you might feel a stronger inclination towards open-mindedness and a desire for social connection. This astrological influence encourages you to embrace your uniqueness and engage in intellectually stimulating conversations shared with others. However, with Mercury forming a square aspect to Jupiter, your communication has the potential for information overload and exaggeration.

**2 Thursday**

Information arrives, opening the door to a fresh start that marks a shift towards expansion, extending the borders of your life. A social aspect shines a light on nurturing friendships, with thoughtful conversations creating an opportunity for companionship. Sharing thoughts and ideas draws well-being and harmony, tapping into a creative vibe that reveals the code to a happy chapter ahead. Expanding your circle of friends brings joy as you connect with others.

**3 Friday**

Openness to meeting new people yields pleasing results, with arriving news offering a favorable aspect for nurturing friendships and companionships. This green light invites engagement with your broader social circle as new possibilities flow into your life. Inspirational conversations become the conduit for sharing insightful ideas and fostering meaningful moments that enrich your well-being and happiness.

**4 Saturday**

You may experience heightened empathy and emotional sensitivity as the Moon moves into Pisces. This astrological influence encourages you to connect with your intuition and explore imagination and creativity. During this lunar transition, you might be more attuned to subtle energies and the emotional undercurrents around you. Pisces' energy fosters a desire for inner reflection and a deeper understanding of your emotions and those of others.

**5 Sunday**

Choices and decisions shape the potential around your life, attracting a journey in connection with your evolving self. Create a sacred space dedicated to nurturing well-being and healing the past, essential for restoring wholeness and harmony. Though you've faced troubles before, your perseverance has made you stronger. By pushing back against roadblocks, you discover a journey that supports your dreams, sweeping away negativity and ushering in transformative change.

**6 Monday**

Your communication may take on a more probing and insightful tone, allowing you to engage in meaningful conversations about profound subjects. Embrace the Aries Moon's drive and the Scorpio Mercury's depth to embark on a dynamic period of action and introspection. This combination encourages you to pursue your goals with determination and explore the depths of your thoughts and emotions, leading to a richer understanding of yourself and the world around you.

**7 Tuesday**

During a Full Moon, you may experience heightened emotions and a sense of culmination. This astrological phase illuminates the hidden, bringing emotions to the surface and offering a chance for deeper self-awareness. However, with Mercury square Pluto, you might also encounter challenges in your communication. This aspect can bring potential power struggles in your conversations. Be mindful of any problematic tendencies in your interactions.

**8 Wednesday**

As the Moon moves into Taurus, you might notice a sense of calm and stability settling over your emotions. This astrological shift encourages you to seek comfort and indulge in simple pleasures. Taurus' energy fosters a connection to the sensual and material aspects of existence, prompting you to find joy in the present moment. Simultaneously, with Venus forming a sextile to Jupiter, your interactions and relationships may experience a boost of positivity and harmony.

**9 Thursday**

Discover equilibrium within the eye of life's storms, cultivating mindfulness even amid the most chaotic weeks. Amidst this chaos, recognize that you tread a path laden with opportunities for growth, learning, and expansion. The news ahead carries the promise of a lighter chapter, prompting a profound shift in focus toward developing your innate talents. Momentum gathers as you unleash your abilities in an environment teeming with possibilities, propelling you toward progression.

**10 Friday**

Moon ingress Gemini. Your emotions become more adaptable and open-minded, allowing you to see different perspectives and consider new ideas. This transition favors exchanging thoughts, sharing information, and expanding your knowledge base. Embrace the Gemini Moon's energy to stimulate your intellect and nurture your social connections, fostering a time of mental exploration and enriched interactions with those around you.

**11 Saturday**

Venus opposed Saturn's astrological aspect, which can bring feelings of isolation, a sense of responsibility, and commitment weighing on your interactions. You might experience barriers to intimacy and find it harder to express affection. However, this opposition also offers an opportunity for growth. It encourages you to address any underlying issues in your relationships honestly and be willing to work through difficulties.

**12 Sunday**

Moon ingress Cancer's astrological influence encourages you to connect with your feelings deeper and seek comfort in familiar surroundings. Cancer's energy fosters a sense of sensitivity and empathy, making it an excellent time to spend quality moments with loved ones and engage in self-care activities that soothe your soul. You might find yourself drawn to home and family matters, valuing a sense of security and emotional connection.

### 13 Monday

As Venus moves into Libra, you may notice a shift towards a desire for harmony and balance in your relationships and surroundings. This astrological transition enhances your appreciation for beauty and aesthetics, prompting you to seek out environments and experiences that evoke a sense of elegance and tranquility. Libra's energy fosters a diplomatic and cooperative atmosphere, encouraging you to find common ground and foster understanding in your interactions with others.

### 14 Tuesday

As the Moon moves into Leo and Venus forms trines to Uranus and Pluto, your emotions become more expressive and dynamic. This combination fosters an opportunity for passionate and transformative connections, potentially bringing shifts in your love life. Embrace the energy of Pluto's direct motion and the harmonious Venus-Uranus and Venus-Pluto trines to navigate with emotional depth and openness, allowing for profound growth and newfound insights.

### 15 Wednesday

A unique path beckons, and expanding horizons with innovative thinking sparks a winning combination, promising pleasing outcomes. Promising signs indicate that you are on track to grow your life outwardly, embracing change and progression with a fresh approach. This exploration allows you to showcase your skills, get your work to a broader audience, and bring valuable rewards that sustain and nurture your spirit.

### 16 Thursday

With the Moon moving into Virgo, you may notice a shift towards a more practical and analytical approach to your emotions. This astrological transition encourages you to focus on details and seek order in your surroundings. Virgo's energy fosters a desire for efficiency and a willingness to take care of tasks. During this lunar transit, you might find satisfaction in organizing and tidying up your environment and focusing on self-improvement and well-being.

**17 Friday**

When the Sun forms a square aspect to Jupiter, you may experience a surge of optimism and enthusiasm. This astrological alignment can bring a sense of expansiveness and a desire to take on new challenges. However, being cautious of overconfidence and the potential for overextending yourself is essential. While this energy can enhance your self-belief and motivation, balancing your ambitions with a practical approach is necessary.

**18 Saturday**

Surprise news invites you out and about, offering a lively social aspect that helps build secure and stable foundations. New possibilities flow into your life, expanding horizons and fueling your confidence to grow and develop. Socializing with your broader circle delivers a wellspring of abundance, emphasizing the importance of nurturing supportive conversations and sharing with companions. Involvement with a social group draws well-being and harmony.

**19 Sunday**

As the Moon moves into Libra, you may see a greater emphasis on harmony and relationships. This astrological transition encourages you to seek balance and cooperation in your interactions with others. Libra's energy fosters fairness and diplomacy, making it an excellent time to engage in discussions and activities that promote understanding. During this lunar transit, you might find yourself drawn to art, culture, aesthetics, and socializing with friends and loved ones.

**20 Monday**

Mercury conjunct Mars. This conjunction can bring abundant mental energy, but it's wise to direct it constructively rather than getting caught up in unnecessary conflicts. Embrace the Mercury-Mars conjunction's power to engage in proactive conversations, initiate new projects, and channel your thoughts into impactful actions while being considerate of others' viewpoints and cultivating a harmonious exchange of ideas.

**21 Tuesday**

New Moon. Moon ingress Scorpio. During a New Moon, you may experience a sense of fresh beginnings and new opportunities. This astrological phase marks the start of a lunar cycle, inviting you to set intentions and embark on a growth journey. As the Moon moves into Scorpio, your emotions may become more intense and transformative. Scorpio's energy encourages you to delve deep within yourself, confronting hidden feelings and seeking profound insights.

**22 Wednesday**

With Neptune moving into Pisces, this astrological transition can bring a sense of empathy and an increased sensitivity to the unseen dimensions of life. Pisces' energy fosters a desire for inner exploration and a greater understanding of the mysteries beyond the material world. You draw artistic and creative pursuits, as Neptune's influence enhances imagination and inspiration. Cultivate unity with the universe and open to beauty beyond the material realm.

**23 Thursday**

Sun ingress Scorpio's astrological transition encourages you to embrace your inner mysteries and delve into the complexities of your emotions and desires. Scorpio's energy fosters a sense of intensity and a willingness to confront both the light and shadow aspects of yourself. This transit is a time for transformation, where you might find yourself drawn to explore psychological depths and engage in self-discovery.

**24 Friday**

As the Moon moves into Sagittarius, you may experience a shift towards a more adventurous and open-minded emotional state. This astrological influence encourages you to seek new experiences, expand your horizons, and embrace a broader perspective on life. However, with the Sun square Pluto, there's potential for intense power struggles and a need to confront hidden truths. This aspect can trigger profound transformations and encourage you to assert your inner strength.

**25 Saturday**

With Mercury forming a trine to Saturn, you may experience a period of enhanced mental discipline and practicality. This astrological alignment empowers you with a clear and structured approach to your thinking and communication. Your ability to focus and pay attention to detail heightens, making it an excellent time for tasks that require concentration and careful planning. This trine fosters a sense of organization and a willingness to tackle responsibilities efficiently.

**26 Sunday**

Moon ingress Capricorn astrological transition encourages you to take a practical and responsible approach to your feelings. Capricorn's energy fosters a sense of discipline and a focus on long-term goals. During this lunar transition, you might be more motivated to tackle tasks requiring persistence. It is when you may prioritize your ambitions and take steps towards achieving them. The Capricorn Moon's influence highlights your resilience and ability to overcome challenges.

### 27 Monday

New information propels you forward in developing an exciting goal, marking a cycle of increasing abundance, magic, and excitement. Life becomes active and progressive, beckoning you to a new area aligned with your current hopes and dreams. Setting sail on a timely voyage, you grow your abilities and work with your talents, reinventing potential and embracing a transition that advances your goals outwardly. Exploring various pathways presents high-level options.

### 28 Tuesday

Mars trines Jupiter. This trine encourages you to step out of your comfort zone and explore new horizons, enhancing self-confidence and assertiveness. It is an opportune time for ventures requiring ambition and calculated risk-taking. Embrace the Mars-Jupiter trine's energy to seize opportunities, progress toward your aspirations, and tap into the abundance of positivity from aligning your efforts with your passions and vision for the future.

### 29 Wednesday

As Mercury enters Sagittarius, your thoughts become more expansive and philosophical. The Mars trine Saturn aspect adds a grounding influence, helping you channel your energy into tasks that require discipline. However, the Mercury-Uranus opposition can bring unexpected changes and disruptions. Use Mercury's energy to connect with like-minded individuals and embrace your quirks while using the Mercury-Neptune trine to express yourself creatively.

### 30 Thursday

With Mercury forming a sextile to Pluto, you may experience a period of enhanced mental clarity and deep insights. This astrological alignment empowers you to delve into complex subjects and uncover hidden truths. Your thinking becomes more focused and wise, allowing you to penetrate beneath the surface and grasp the underlying dynamics of situations. This sextile encourages meaningful conversations and the potential for transformative ideas.

# NOVEMBER

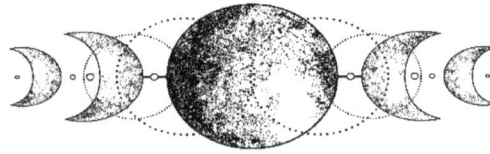

MOON MAGIC

| Sun | Mon | Tue | Wed | Thu | Fri | Sat |
|-----|-----|-----|-----|-----|-----|-----|
|     |     |     |     |     |     | 1   |
| 2   | 3   | 4   | 5   | 6   | 7   | 8   |
| 9   | 10  | 11  | 12  | 13  | 14  | 15  |
| 16  | 17  | 18  | 19  | 20  | 21  | 22  |
| 23  | 24  | 25  | 26  | 27  | 28  | 29  |
| 30  |     |     |     |     |     |     |

# NEW MOON

# BEAVER MOON

**31 Friday**

As the Moon moves into Pisces, you may notice a shift towards a more sensitive and intuitive emotional state. This astrological transition encourages you to connect with your inner world and deeply embrace your emotions. Pisces' energy fosters a sense of empathy and compassion, urging you to tune into the feelings of others as well. During this lunar transit, you might find solace in creative activities or moments of quiet reflection.

**1 Saturday**

Receiving information allows you to cross the threshold into a brighter chapter, focusing on developing goals to improve your well-being and nurture your spirit. A changing scene on the horizon brings a reinvigorating social aspect, ushering in an active and happy chapter of engaging with the broader world. A windfall of abundance takes you on a journey forward, inviting you to mingle and network with kindred spirits, building solid foundations in your social life.

**2 Sunday**

Venus square Jupiter aspect can bring forth a desire for extravagance or a tendency to overlook practical considerations. While the Aries Moon's energy encourages you to seize the moment, balancing your enthusiasm with a mindful approach to relationships and decision-making is essential. Use this combination to navigate the day with purpose and vigor while exercising caution and considering the consequences of your actions and choices.

**3 Monday**

Crafting your vision and planning for the future yields a pleasing result, marking a significant turning point with skyrocketing potential in your world. Expansion and progression rule this time, and strategic planning is essential for informed, proactive steps toward growing the path ahead. Dabbling and evolving in new topics chart a course toward a journey filled with creative inspiration, significant change, and rising prospects.

**4 Tuesday**

The Mars-opposed Uranus aspect introduces an element of unpredictability and potential disruptions. Embrace the Mars-Neptune trine's energy to blend your dreams with practicality, using intuition to guide actions. As Mars enters Sagittarius, engage in experiences that broaden horizons while the Taurus Moon encourages you to create a nurturing environment. With the Mars-Uranus opposition, stay open and adaptable as you navigate dynamic energies.

**5 Wednesday**

Full Moon. Emotions may run high during this phase, and you could experience heightened awareness about your desires and needs. It's an opportune moment to release what no longer serves you and to set intentions for the upcoming lunar cycle. The energy of the Full Moon invites you to find harmony between your external actions and your inner feelings, promoting personal growth and transformation.

**6 Thursday**

With Mars forming a sextile to Pluto, you may experience increased determination. This astrological alignment empowers you to channel your energy into transformative actions. As the Moon moves into Gemini, your emotions may become more adaptable and communicative. Venus entering Scorpio adds intensity to your relationships and desires. This combination encourages you to explore deeper emotional connections and engage in meaningful conversations.

**7 Friday**

Constructive dialogues create a lively and expressive time of sharing thoughts with kindred spirits, enticing new possibilities. A happy shift enchants your world with refreshing options. Refreshing news sparks a transition, aligning you with a change of pace and a social time filled with happiness and joy. Attracting new potential it rejuvenates and renews inspiration, drawing abundance into your world in a productive and lively chapter.

**8 Saturday**

As Uranus moves into Taurus, you may enter a period of significant shifts and innovations. As the Moon moves into Cancer, your emotions become more nurturing and sensitive. This combination invites you to seek comfort in familiar surroundings and connect with your innermost feelings. Embrace Uranus in Taurus' energy to adapt to new financial and value-based paradigms while using the Venus-Pluto square as a catalyst for growth.

**9 Sunday**

Mercury's retrograde astrological phase encourages you to slow down and review your thoughts, communication, and plans. During this time, you might experience a sense of revisiting past situations or reconsidering decisions you've made. Mercury's retrograde motion can sometimes bring challenges in communication and technology, so it's wise to exercise patience and double-check details before making essential commitments.

### 10 Monday

As the Moon moves into Leo, you may notice a shift towards a more expressive and vibrant emotional state. This astrological transition encourages you to embrace your creativity and seek opportunities for self-expression. Leo's energy fosters a desire to shine and be recognized, urging you to engage in activities that bring you joy and allow you to showcase your unique talents. During this lunar transit, you enjoy social interactions and activities that make you feel special.

### 11 Tuesday

Jupiter turns retrograde. It's a time for focusing on self-improvement, gaining a deeper understanding of your motivations, and making any necessary adjustments to your long-term plans. Embrace the Jupiter retrograde energy to reflect on your journey, expand your inner horizons, and develop a more authentic and meaningful sense of purpose as you navigate this internal exploration and self-discovery period.

### 12 Wednesday

With Mercury forming a conjunction with Mars, you may experience intensified mental energy and assertiveness. This astrological alignment empowers you to communicate your thoughts and ideas with vigor and determination. Your mind becomes more focused and quick to take action. As the Moon moves into Virgo, your emotions may become more practical and detail-oriented. This combination encourages you to engage in tasks that require precision.

### 13 Thursday

The wheel turns as you venture into uncharted territory and research a new area of interest. Broadening your horizons explores leads, awakening a rich landscape of potential that nurtures your talents, symbolizing a period of expansive growth and profound transformation. Rising potency and manifestation enrich a significant turning point in your life, drawing an enterprising path forward and indicating a chapter of unprecedented possibilities and achievements.

### 14 Friday

Feeling in sync with your circle of friends, a sense of connection lifts the lid on lively discussions and group bonding sessions, heightening creativity through brainstorming and engagement. Triggering a path that nurtures well-being and harmony, this phase of life becomes more balanced as you lay the groundwork for a stable and secure home environment. Deepening friendships encourages an optimistic outlook and creates a time tailor-made for sharing discussions.

### 15 Saturday

Moon ingress Libra. During this lunar transition, you might crave social activities and engage in conversations that create understanding and unity. Your aesthetic sensibilities may heighten, inspiring you to appreciate beauty and engage in artistic pursuits. Embrace the Libra Moon's energy to foster meaningful connections, create an atmosphere of grace, and seek the shared values that bring people together in a spirit of mutual respect and collaboration.

### 16 Sunday

Unforeseen changes on the horizon empower you to dismantle barriers, constructing a sturdy bridge toward a brighter future. This juncture heralds significant developments in your life, unveiling fresh possibilities that beckon you forward. Social engagement takes center stage, fostering lively discussions, a flurry of activities, and heightened social attention, paving the way for growth and rejuvenation. Insightful conversations bring excitement and novel ideas.

### 17 Monday

With the Sun forming trines to Jupiter and Saturn, you may experience a period of balanced expansion and disciplined growth. These cosmic trines encourage you to take confident steps toward your goals, aided by optimism and discipline. With Mercury sextile Pluto, your communication may take on a more profound and insightful quality. As the Moon moves into Scorpio, your emotions may become more intense and introspective.

### 18 Tuesday

Revealing improvement brings grounded energy that smooths out bumps, reaching a turning point. Encouragement on the horizon guides you towards a soul-affirming and rewarding journey. Exploring various avenues opens a way that brings a shift toward growth, promising a fulfilling trajectory. Creating space to nurture your life draws stability and balance, clearing the deck to explore new areas and develop your abilities.

### 19 Wednesday

As Mercury moves into Scorpio, you may enter a period of intensified thoughts and communication. This astrological transition encourages you to delve deep into matters that intrigue you, seeking to uncover hidden truths and deeper meanings. The Mercury-opposed Uranus aspect can bring unexpected disruptions in your thinking and conversations, urging you to remain flexible and open to innovative ideas.

### 20 Thursday

During a New Moon, you may experience a fresh start and a sense of new beginnings. This astrological phase marks a time of setting intentions and planting seeds for future growth. With the Sun conjunct Mercury, your thoughts and communication align with your aspirations. As Mercury moves into Sagittarius, your thinking becomes more expansive and open to new perspectives. The Uranus sextile Neptune aspect adds a touch of creative inspiration and spiritual insight.

### 21 Friday

As the Sun opposes Uranus, you may experience unexpected changes and desire freedom. Embrace the Sun's opposition to Uranus as an opportunity to embrace change and a more liberated perspective while allowing the Sun's trine to Neptune to guide you in channeling your desires into meaningful and compassionate endeavors. This period encourages you to balance your need for personal expression and your ability to connect with others on a deeper, intuitive level.

### 22 Saturday

With the Sun moving into Sagittarius, you may feel a shift towards a more adventurous and optimistic energy. This astrological transition encourages you to embrace a broader perspective. As Mercury forms a trine to Saturn, your thinking becomes focused, allowing you to approach tasks with attention to detail. With the Moon moving into Capricorn, your emotions may become more serious and responsible, motivating you to set goals and work diligently towards them.

### 23 Sunday

With the Sun forming a sextile to Pluto, you may experience increased personal power and transformative potential. This astrological alignment empowers you to tap into your inner strength and make positive changes in your life. The Sun's sextile to Pluto encourages you to dig deep into your motivations and embrace your capacity for growth and renewal. This aspect can empower you to shed light on hidden aspects and make constructive shifts.

### 24 Monday

Exciting news lays the groundwork for future goals, allowing you to plan strategically for a brighter future. A new role brings a lead ripe for development, connecting you with expansion and progression, highlighting a phase of growing your abilities, utilizing your gifts, and positively changing the foundations of your life. New information links you to a creative project, sparking discussions with your circle of friends and fostering an atmosphere of creativity and collaboration.

### 25 Tuesday

Mercury conjunct Venus. Moon ingress Aquarius. This combination encourages you to engage with your community and explore innovative ideas. Embrace the Mercury-Venus conjunction's energy to express your thoughts gracefully while the Aquarius Moon invites you to connect with like-minded individuals. Use this cosmic interplay to foster connections and contribute to group endeavors while remaining open to diverse perspectives and intellectual exploration.

### 26 Wednesday

With Venus forming trines to Jupiter and Saturn, you may experience a period of harmonious and balanced energy in matters of love, relationships, and creativity. This astrological alignment empowers you with a sense of abundance and stability. The Venus trine Jupiter aspect brings an atmosphere of optimism and expansion, potentially leading to fortunate opportunities in your social or romantic life.

### 27 Thursday

Pisces' energy fosters a sense of unity and a desire to create a warm and nurturing atmosphere. Whether you're spending the day with family or friends, this lunar influence invites you to express gratitude and love and to create an environment where everyone feels cherished. Allow the Pisces Moon's energy to inspire heartfelt conversations and shared understanding as you celebrate Thanksgiving with emotional closeness and appreciation for the bonds you share.

**28 Friday**

Saturn's direct astrological phenomenon signifies when the challenges and lessons associated with Saturn's retrograde phase begin moving forward. It's a period for taking the wisdom you've gained during Saturn's retrograde and applying it to your life more tangibly. Saturn's direct motion encourages you to take responsibility, set boundaries, and continue working steadily towards your ambitions.

**29 Saturday**

With Mercury moving forward, you'll likely notice greater clarity in your thoughts, more fluid communication, and a smoother flow in your everyday activities. It's an excellent time to revisit any plans or decisions that may have been put on hold and to move with a clearer sense of direction. This direct motion encourages you to apply the insights you've gained during the retrograde period, helping you make well-informed choices and confidently progress.

**30 Sunday**

With Venus entering Sagittarius, your approach to love and desires may become more adventurous and open-minded. Embrace the Aries Moon's energy to make bold moves and express your individuality while using the Venus aspects to navigate any relationship surprises with empathy and creativity. Let Venus in Sagittarius inspire you to explore new horizons in love and approach your desires with optimism and enthusiasm as you navigate this dynamic period.

# December

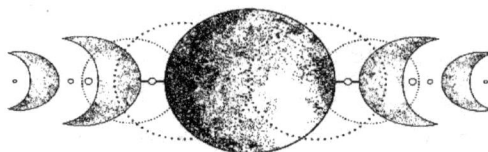

MOON MAGIC

| Sun | Mon | Tue | Wed | Thu | Fri | Sat |
|-----|-----|-----|-----|-----|-----|-----|
|     | 1   | 2   | 3   | 4   | 5   | 6   |
| 7   | 8   | 9   | 10  | 11  | 12  | 13  |
| 14  | 15  | 16  | 17  | 18  | 19  | 20  |
| 21  | 22  | 23  | 24  | 25  | 26  | 27  |
| 28  | 29  | 30  | 31  |     |     |     |

# New Moon

# COLD MOON

# DECEMBER

### 1 Monday

As your proficiency in your craft grows, so does your confidence, propelling you towards new opportunities that promise expansion in various aspects of your life. This pathway of growth holds the key to rising prospects, urging you to develop your talents and extend your abilities into uncharted territories. A new role emerges, allowing your gifts to reach a broader audience and bringing a fresh chapter of possibilities.

### 2 Tuesday

With the Moon moving into Taurus, you may feel a shift towards a more grounded and practical emotional state. This astrological transition encourages you to seek comfort, stability, and sensual pleasures. Taurus' energy fosters a desire for security and a connection to the material world. Additionally, the Venus sextile Pluto aspect adds intensity and depth to your relationships and passions, inviting you to explore the deeper layers of your connections.

### 3 Wednesday

Engaging consistently with your talents advances your gifts to the next level, emphasizing the importance of daily practice for studying, researching, and developing your abilities. Your commitment to enhancing your skills bears fruit, and being open to unique pathways unfolds a life in an eclectic direction. As you paint the backdrop of your vision for future growth, you discover ample room to extend and refine your abilities.

### 4 Thursday

This Full Moon invites you to embrace your rational and emotional sides, balancing your thoughts and feelings. It's a time to express yourself, connect with those around you, and gather information that can lead to a deeper understanding of your experiences. As the light of the Full Moon illuminates your world, use this period to reflect, make decisions, and release what no longer serves you as you navigate this heightened mental and emotional awareness phase.

### 5 Friday

As the element of surprise expands your horizons, new people enter your life, enabling you to spread your wings and enjoy an active and energetic social life filled with bright blessings. Engaging in a community project replenishes inspiration, sparking a creative phase that connects with kindred spirits and offers friendships and social activities promoting well-being and happiness. This journey lands you in a refreshing environment, unveiling new possibilities.

### 6 Saturday

You might notice a more nurturing and emotional atmosphere as the Moon moves into Cancer. This astrological transition encourages you to seek comfort in familiar settings and connect with your innermost feelings. Cancer's energy fosters a desire for emotional security and a deeper connection to your home and loved ones. Additionally, with Mercury forming a trine to Neptune, your thoughts and communication take on a more intuitive and compassionate quality.

### 7 Sunday

You are lifting the lid on a fresh start, ushering in a positive influence, creating space for your creativity to shine as you establish your talents in a unique area. The potent mix of manifestation and inspiration brings the wind of change, allowing you to build a grounded foundation for your dreams. This happy chapter unfolds with expansion and harmony, witnessing an increase in your social life. It lights a busy path forward toward a remarkable destination.

**8 Monday**

Creating space to nurture your talents initiates a positive shift, marking a significant turning point. This journey offers insights into future possibilities, driven by a richly creative process. Exploring these options allows you to refine your gifts and work with your abilities, unveiling a unique landscape that beckons you forward as new priorities take shape. Abundance becomes a resonant theme as you explore pathways with rising prospects, providing a fresh start.

**9 Tuesday**

With Mars forming a square to Saturn, you might face challenges and obstacles that test your patience and determination. This astrological aspect can bring about a sense of frustration and limitations in your actions and desires. It's essential to be cautious and avoid taking impulsive risks during this period, as the square suggests potential roadblocks or delays in your pursuits. However, the Mars-Saturn square also offers an opportunity for disciplined effort and persistence.

**10 Wednesday**

With the Moon moving into Virgo, you may experience a more practical and analytical emotional state. This astrological transition encourages you to focus on details and routines, and it can be an ideal time for organization and tidying up loose ends. Additionally, with Neptune turning direct, you might notice a subtle shift in your intuitive and spiritual awareness. Neptune's direct motion can bring clarity and a deeper connection to your dreams and inner wisdom.

**11 Thursday**

With Mercury forming a trine to Neptune, you may experience heightened intuition and imaginative thinking. This astrological alignment empowers you to communicate with empathy and connect with your inner wisdom. Your thoughts take on a more dreamy and compassionate quality, making it a suitable time for artistic and spiritual pursuits. As Mercury moves into Sagittarius, your thinking becomes more expansive and open to new ideas and philosophies.

**12 Friday**

Moon ingress Libra astrological transition encourages fairness and cooperation in your interactions. Libra's energy fosters a desire for companionship and a willingness to find common ground. During this lunar transit, you might find yourself drawn to social activities and engaging in conversations that create understanding and unity. Your sense of aesthetics may also be heightened, inspiring you to appreciate the beauty in your surroundings.

**13 Saturday**

Mercury's sextile Pluto aspect can enhance your ability to uncover hidden truths and tap into your inner wisdom. Use this cosmic synergy to engage in discussions that promote personal growth and allow for the sharing of powerful insights. Embrace the Mercury-Pluto sextile's energy to foster a deeper connection to your thoughts and the world around you, enabling you to navigate this period with a sense of mental empowerment and a desire to explore the profound.

**14 Sunday**

Mars square Neptune. This period may require you to step back, reevaluate your goals, and be mindful of any deceptive influences or hidden agendas in your interactions. Embrace the Mars-Neptune square as an opportunity to develop self-awareness and consider your actions' true motivations. It's a time to proceed with caution, trust your intuition, and avoid making hasty decisions until the fog of confusion fades.

**15 Monday**

As the Moon enters Scorpio, you might sense a deepening of emotions and a heightened intensity in your inner world. This astrological transition encourages you to delve beneath the surface and explore the profound layers of your feelings and desires. Scorpio's energy fosters a natural inclination to uncover hidden truths and transform aspects of your life. Additionally, with Mars moving into Capricorn, your actions become more disciplined and strategic.

**16 Tuesday**

An influx of information cascades into your life, ushering in a wealth of options that facilitate progressive movement toward unique goals. Positive change is spurred by good news, sparking an exploration of pathways and unearthing leads. Lighter energy envelops your journey, bringing a sunny aspect infused with blessings. The climate becomes ripe with potential, and remaining open to new possibilities draws tangible results.

**17 Wednesday**

Sun square Saturn's astrological aspect can bring challenges and obstacles that test your resolve and demand a disciplined approach. It may feel like your ambitions are met with resistance, and you could grapple with self-doubt or limitations. However, as the Moon moves into Sagittarius, there's an opportunity for a shift in perspective. This lunar transition encourages you to embrace a more optimistic and adventurous outlook.

**18 Thursday**

An original opportunity emerges, inviting you into a game-changing journey of advancement and progression. Planning your trajectory becomes the key, ushering in innovative options aligned with growing talents, ultimately bringing fruitful results and a chance to share your work with a broader audience. Moving away from areas that limit progress cracks the code to a brighter chapter, as incoming news injects a welcomed boost into your life.

## 19 Friday

Changes ahead bring an abundant chapter to light, nurturing your spirit by drawing rejuvenating energy into your life. This phase helps grow social engagement and boost magic in your wider community environment, offering stable foundations that promote balance and harmony. Opportunities to mingle kick off an energetic time of lively discussions and entertaining conversations. It fuels the fires of inspiration as you share with others who offer bright ideas.

## 20 Saturday

The New Moon astrological phase marks a time for planting seeds of intention, making it favorable to initiate projects or start afresh in various areas of your life. As the Moon moves into Capricorn, you'll find a grounded and disciplined energy prevailing, encouraging you to approach your goals with determination and a strategic mindset. Additionally, the Black Moon's ingress into Sagittarius adds an element of mystery and depth to your quest for knowledge and spiritual growth.

## 21 Sunday

With the Sun forming a square to Neptune, you might find a sense of confusion and ambiguity clouding your direction. This astrological aspect can create a fog that blurs perceptions and makes it challenging to discern reality from illusion. Concurrently, the Venus square to Saturn can bring a sense of limitation and responsibility to your relationships and finances. It may feel like barriers or coldness in matters of the heart or personal resources.

### 22 Monday

Moon ingress Aquarius astrological transition encourages you to embrace individuality and uniquely engage with your social circle and community. Aquarius' energy fosters a desire for innovation and a willingness to explore unconventional ideas and experiences. During this lunar phase, you might find yourself drawn to humanitarian causes and a sense of camaraderie with like-minded individuals.

### 23 Tuesday

An emphasis on improving life opens a fresh slate of potential, bringing a self-expressive time that promotes social engagement and communication. Sharing thoughts and ideas with your broader circle creates curious thoughts, offering a blueprint for future development. Crafting your vision for the future brings an environment showcasing your talents, attracting wellness and abundance in a supportive environment that blesses your life.

### 24 Wednesday

Venus square Neptune. Venus ingress Capricorn. This transition encourages you to approach your relationships and financial matters with a sense of responsibility and a focus on long-term stability. While the Venus-Neptune square may bring uncertainty, the Capricorn Venus invites you to take a structured and disciplined approach to your desires and resources, allowing you to navigate this period with wisdom and a commitment to building solid foundations.

### 25 Thursday

As the Moon gracefully moves into Pisces on Christmas Day, you may be enveloped in a dreamy and compassionate atmosphere. This astrological transition encourages you to embrace the spirit of the holiday season, where empathy, love, and goodwill prevail. Pisces' energy fosters a deep connection to your emotions and an intuitive understanding of the needs of others. It's a time for kindness, reflection, and a heightened sense of unity with those you cherish.

**26 Friday**

Positive news arrives, setting conditions ripe for growth, security, and stability, improving your bottom line. Developing and advancing life leads to refreshing options and linking up with friends to create a community environment. Engaging in activities with kindred spirits and sharing thoughts with supportive people offers a trailblazing chapter that promotes creativity. The strong emphasis on improving circumstances culminates in a journey offering expansive horizons.

**27 Saturday**

Aries' energy fosters a sense of independence and a willingness to confront challenges head-on. You may be more inclined to assert your needs and enthusiastically tackle tasks during this time. It's an opportune moment to start new projects and channel your emotional energy into productive endeavors. Use this cosmic influence to ignite your passions and fuel your ambitions, allowing your inner fire to drive you toward your goals and inspirations with vigor.

**28 Sunday**

Life's transformational phase brings exciting developments and a chance to mingle with friends, leading to a journey offering growth and rising prospects. Nurturing unique friendships blesses your world, igniting inspiration and fostering a connected and supportive vibe that provides well-being and harmony. This phase also creates space to work with your creative abilities and develop plans for future growth, shaping a rejuvenating and transformative expansion.

**29 Monday**

With the Moon's gentle transition into Taurus, you may experience a sense of stability and groundedness in your emotions and surroundings. This astrological shift encourages you to seek comfort, security, and a connection to the physical world. Taurus' energy fosters a desire for simplicity and a slower, more deliberate pace of life. You might appreciate life's pleasures, from indulging in delicious food to taking in the beauty of the natural world.

**30 Tuesday**

When Mercury squares Saturn, you might encounter challenges communicating and processing information. This aspect can make it feel like your thoughts and ideas are constantly met with resistance or obstacles. Your mind may be more critical and analytical, leading to self-doubt and a tendency to overthink things. It's essential to balance your desire for structure and precision and your need for open communication.

**31 Wednesday**

Moon ingress Gemini. Gemini is an air sign known for its curiosity and versatility, and this lunar placement can make you feel more communicative, pleasant, and mentally active as you ring in the new year. You may be eager to converse, connect with others, and explore various ideas and interests. It's a time for light-hearted celebrations or simply enjoying the company of friends and loved ones as you welcome the year ahead with curiosity and adaptability.

**1 Thursday**

On New Year's Day, Mercury's ingress into Capricorn, combined with a challenging square to Neptune, may bring about a somewhat perplexing start to the year for you. While Mercury in Capricorn can enhance your practical thinking and goal-setting abilities, the square aspect with Neptune could cloud your judgment and introduce confusion into your thought processes. You may need to navigate a fine line between ambition and idealism.

# Astrology, Tarot & Horoscope Books.

Mystic Cat

**Mystic Cat Tqrot**

In Relationship Reading
$15.00

Crossroads
$10.00

Next Relationship Reading
$15.00

Ohoroscope@Hotmail.com

www.ingramcontent.com/pod-product-compliance
Lightning Source LLC
Chambersburg PA
CBHW080531090426
42733CB00015B/2546